the
GARDENING
IN
MINIATURE
prop shop

the
GARDENING
IN
MINIATURE
prop shop

Handmade Accessories for
Your Tiny Living World

JANIT CALVO

with photographs by Kate Baldwin

TIMBER PRESS
Portland, Oregon

For my Mom and Dad, who planted the
seeds of art, craft, gardening, and miniatures

Published in 2017 by Timber Press, Inc.
The Haseltine Building
133 S.W. Second Avenue, Suite 450
Portland, Oregon 97204-3527
timberpress.com

Printed in China
Text and cover design by Laken Wright

Library of Congress Cataloging-in-Publication Data

Names: Calvo, Janit, author.
Title: The gardening in miniature prop shop: handmade accessories for your tiny
    living world / Janit Calvo; with photographs by Kate Baldwin.
Description: Portland, Oregon: Timber Press, 2017. | Includes bibliographical
    references and index.
Identifiers: LCCN 2016045507 (print) | LCCN 2017005197 (ebook) | ISBN
    9781604697018 (pbk.) | ISBN 9781604698091 (e-book)
Subjects: LCSH: Gardens, Miniature. | Garden ornaments and furniture. | Garden
    structures.
Classification: LCC SB433.5 .C37125 2017 (print) | LCC SB433.5 (ebook) | DDC
    635.9--dc23
LC record available at https://lccn.loc.gov/2016045507

ISBN 13: 978-1-60469-701-8
A catalog record for this book is also available from the British Library.

CONTENTS

GETTING STARTED　11

WORLD TOUR　29

MAKE IT SPECIAL　81

MINIATURE IMAGININGS 145

BEYOND THE MINIATURE GARDEN 203

INTRODUCTION

There is no other pastime as diverse, adaptable, and accessible as gardening in miniature. It is a collection of a number of other hobbies merged into a single incredibly creative one. And it appears that we've taken the best and easiest aspects of these leisure pursuits and left the hardest parts of them behind.

We don't break our backs gardening and landscaping: we use spoons for shovels, forks for rakes, and we find ways to grow slow and small. We play with plants *and* with the garden. We casually build small hills and dales in our gardens; we effortlessly carve riverbeds and move property boundaries on a whim. We dream of different ways to plant and repurpose tiny plots morning, noon, and night. We begin a fresh garden design from scratch with every new pot we pick up, or every garden bed we till, something full-size gardeners simply cannot do.

We can appreciate all kinds of miniature and dwarf plants and include leggy shrubs and broken trees in our work because we will use them as authentic additions to our miniature garden scenes. We adore tiny conifers with their little buds and needles not as collectors, but because they are genuine landscape trees in miniature.

We don't practice the art of bonsai, but we will gladly use its ancient techniques for pruning and looking at plants in a new way. We use the same bonsai-tree starts but instead of cropping off the roots to fit them into shallow trays, we lovingly place them, uncut root ball and all,

into our miniature gardens as delicious anchor trees and hang tiny swings or birdhouses from them.

Instead of spending hours indoors renovating a dollhouse, we take our miniatures outside and put them in the soil. We can complete a garden from start to finish in a couple of hours; that's a feat seldom heard of in the dollhouse world. We don't craft just anything and everything either; our projects have to rev up our imaginations, fill our hearts, fit into our tiny gardens, and be special enough to warrant giving up such valuable real estate.

We are versatile crafters as long as it has something to do with the miniature garden. We dabble in masonry, mosaics, woodworking, painting, and all kinds of applied arts. We love to use our hands and minds to build and make rather than just buy an idea to plunk down in a pot of soil. We relish the realistic details, knowing that that is where the magic and enchantment is made.

We can't join an established club because we would be guilty of being so selective. If a miniature gardener were looking for a club to join, which would it be? A dollhouse-miniature club would quickly scale down any idea made with living plants, real soil, and water. A rock garden club would toss us out for aggregating with trees and miniatures. A conifer or a regular garden club would consider us weeds because we would only attend when the topic resonates in miniature. A bonsai group would prune us away for sneaking in miniature patios and

Miniature gardeners garden as little as possible.

practical in application, and will delight the novice and experienced miniature gardener alike. In other words, you don't need that specific chair in the project to do the project; interpret the projects for your own ideas. Have fun, make mistakes, and create.

This book begins with advice for setting up the ideal workshop for a miniature gardener and an overview of the basic materials and tools needed for most projects. Then we move on to the projects, which range from nationally themed projects capturing the spirit of Great Britain, Spain, Japan, and India to projects inspired by special occasions, from the Fourth of July and Halloween to birthdays and weddings. Storybook ideas follow: a fairy house, an intriguing door to the world of gnomes, a shack on a deserted island, aliens from outer space, and a world beneath the sea. And last, we look at Wardian cases and broken-pot gardening, and sneak attacks (okay, with permission) in the form of guerrilla gardening.

With all the projects in this book, let your imagination fly. Reinvent or adapt the ideas to use with other themes. Take the techniques gathered here and use them with abandon. Each project is photographed in a miniature garden to show you how the finished piece looks in a garden and to give you an idea of how you might apply it to your own gardens. I hope you'll enjoy this book as much as I enjoyed getting my ideas out of my head and onto these pages.

furniture under their specimens. Railroad garden groups would put us on the next train out because we would only want to talk about the plants and the garden.

So, here is another book for you, my fellow miniature gardener: you are welcome in this club anytime. This book is a follow-up to my first book, *Gardening in Miniature: Create Your Own Tiny Living World*. Grow, play, experiment, plant, create, invent, dig in deeper, or garden smaller anytime. But do think big and dream bigger.

My goal for this book is to offer unique projects that are doable by anyone, independent of their skill level, are

GETTING STARTED

CREATING A MINIATURE GARDEN WORKSHOP

The ideal workshop for the serious miniature gardener would consist of three separate workspaces. The first would be an outdoor area for storing plants and containers, planting, and getting dirty. This area would have a potting bench to work on and shelves to keep the plants and gardens off the ground, which makes it easy to water and care for them.

The second area would be for doing custom patio work, where you can keep all your stone and tile pieces handy and in view so they will not be overlooked, and where you can make a mess. This is where you would keep a plastic tub for Mini Patio Mix, and where you would keep a handy mister bottle handy, too.

The third area would be a comfortable spot for your mini-making: a clean, warm, dry, and well-lit place to sit down and create, customize, paint, and repair the accessories for your miniature gardens.

And if you are seriously serious about miniature gardening, the ideal workspace would include a jeweler's workbench. Jeweler's workbenches are designed to hold the project you're working on at eye level, so that you're not sitting hunched over for long periods of time. They usually have a number of small drawers, slots, and compartments to store tools and supplies, and a railing around the edge to prevent tools and supplies from rolling off.

A workshop of one's own: a spot to create in can be inspirational in itself.

A Temporary Miniature Garden Workshop

Having an area to make a mess in and not have to clean it up immediately afterward is critical for the creative process to occur. It typically takes the human brain a minimum of 20 minutes to refocus on a task after being distracted. Add that to the amount of time spent unpacking supplies and tools, setting up a work area, and repacking and cleaning up afterward every time you work on a project, and you've lost valuable creative time and quite possibly the initial creative spark that started the process in the first place.

Since many miniature gardeners don't have enough space to set up a permanent workshop, a work-around is setting up a temporary studio that can be used for a weekend, a few days, or even a month so that you can work on a long project, or several short projects, and not have to clean up right away. Pushing the couch back and spreading an old sheet on the floor and getting creatively messy for a few days feels liberating, and it's equally satisfying to return the space to its usual condition after you are done, too.

Miniature Gardening in Your Kitchen

Miniature gardening is very adaptable. You do not have to commit any space or, for that matter, any length of time to the hobby. You can easily set up projects on your

Create a spot to
make a mess for
more fun.

A little paint goes a long way in the miniature studio.

kitchen table or counter and create for an afternoon. Here are some pointers to help you get started:

Protect the work surface properly. Cover your kitchen table or counter with cardboard to protect it from getting scratched.

Designate a bigger workspace than you need, or use a drop cloth or an old sheet to cover up appliances and any food that's stored on the counter. Sand and soil tend to travel when you're potting up plants in the kitchen. You can contain the soil and make cleanup a breeze at the same time.

If you keep your miniature garden session on the dry side, it will be much easier to clean up rather than deal with mud.

When you're finished working, sterilize the kitchen counter and sink before you use it to prepare food.

Keep your mini-garden fork and spoon tools separate from your other cutlery, or make sure you wash them well before using them to eat or prepare food.

The Mini Miniature Garden Studio

If you're a dedicated miniature gardener and you live in a small space but want a permanent area in which to work,

try setting up a work area in a corner that has enough room for a cupboard or shelves. With a few attractive storage containers, you can create a space that is both functional and looks good with your other furnishings. On open shelves, use covered boxes and baskets to hide the messiest supplies. Tools and paintbrushes can look artsy in a container on the corner of a desk. Make sure to have some good lighting; you will need to see the small details. Luxo lamps are ideal and there are more options available at your local craft store, too. Think about floor lamps if your table space is limited, and keep in mind that some craft lamps come with a built-in magnifier that is meant for needlework but can easily solve the lighting problems of a miniature gardener.

Tools and supplies for miniature gardening are as varied as the hobby.

TOOLS, MATERIALS, AND TECHNIQUES

Having the right tools is essential to successful mini-making; they'll help you work through each step with ease and make your projects look polished. The tools and supplies for miniature gardening vary as much as the hobby does and can be found at your local hardware store, craft store, garden center, florist, or online. This chapter includes lists of tools and supplies that are helpful to have on hand.

You'll need heavy-duty and craft scissors.

Basic Tools

Garden clippers

Small spade or trenching tool

Fork

Spoon

Scissors (three pairs: heavy-duty, regular, and small)

Small hammer

Tweezers, large and small

Dry paintbrush for sweeping

Pump spray or mister

Watering can

Kneeler

Clamps, large and small

Hardware cloth

Wood border strips

Metal rods in different widths, straight floral wire, or welding rod

Wood skewers

Floral wire, two kinds:

- Straight, for staking unusual items or making garden art
- Spooled, for wrapping and creating twig fences, trellises, and arbors

Toothbrush, for cleaning tiny details

Windex, for cleaning up the exterior of garden containers

Clean, soft rags

Find different colors of floral wire in your local craft store.

Safety and Protection

GARDENING GLOVES Protect your hands and skin whenever you can by wearing gloves. A rubber-on-cotton design holds up well. The rubber makes it easy to grip pots and tools firmly, making them invaluable for moving around plants and containers. They can be tossed in the washing machine when they're dirty. Wash them inside out if they get really smelly.

LEATHER GLOVES Leather gloves are ideal for working in the workshop, especially when you're drilling miniature pieces. If the drill slips and hits your hand, the leather may be able to deflect the drill bit to provide some protection.

SAFETY GLASSES Wear eye protection when you're breaking up marble and tile for your miniature garden patios and pathways, or for any task that sends shards flying. Get a full-face mask as well as a pair of safety glasses for lighter jobs. Never take a chance with your eyes; after all, you only get two per lifetime!

LATEX GLOVES Disposable latex gloves are handy for messy painting jobs. They can be gently reused a couple of times before they'll need to be discarded.

Get good-quality tools and they will last a lifetime. Left to right: tile snips, linesman's pliers, hammer.

A sledgehammer and chisel are indispensable for breaking up marble tile.

HEAVY-DUTY RUBBER GLOVES These are tougher than latex gloves, and perfect for big messy projects like cleaning out garden containers and pots.

Workshop Tools

SMALL SLEDGEHAMMER AND CHISEL You'll need a sledgehammer and chisel for breaking up large pieces of flagstone or marble tile. Look for a chisel with a protective shield on the handle. The shield saves you from worrying about accidentally hitting your hand with the sledgehammer. If you are not comfortable using a small sledgehammer, then a regular hammer will do.

JEWELRY PLIERS You can usually find a set of jewelry pliers that has different kinds of needle-nose and flat-nose pliers with wire snips. Make sure the set includes round-nose pliers; you'll need them to make wire tendrils and shepherd hooks.

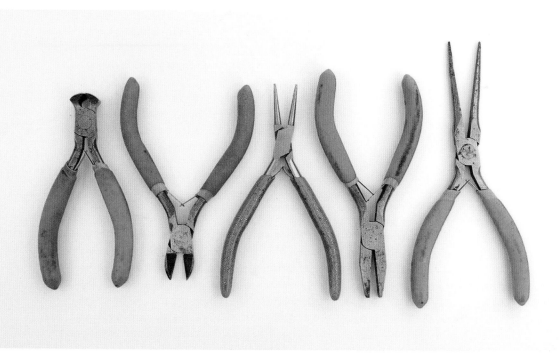

From left to right: end cutters, diagonal cutters, round-nose pliers, flat-nose pliers, and long needle-nose pliers.

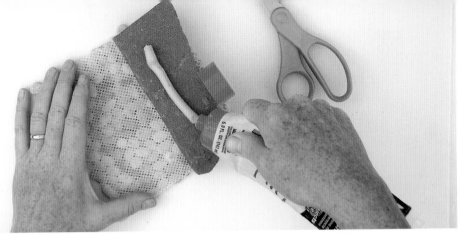

Choosing the right glue for your project is an important consideration, especially for projects that will live outdoors.

Adhesives

Adhesives are an essential part of the miniature garden workshop. It's important to have a variety of adhesives on hand for the different requirements of the hobby because all adhesives are not equal when you're working in miniature. For some applications, like drilling and staking resin accessories, you'll need to leave space in the drilled hole for the epoxy glue so that there is room for the glue to adhere to both the stake and the accessory. For other applications, where you would like the glue to be hidden, use a thinner glue, like superglue, for example. (You will learn several ways to hide the glue from view in this book.) Hot glue is a bulky, thick glue that is visible in the join after it dries. Before you begin a project, take a moment to consider the result you want, then choose which glue to use.

TWO-PART EPOXY Epoxy has a strong bond that dries clear, but it can yellow outdoors. It's a strong glue for resin, plastic, stone, glass, and other materials. It has a great resistance to weather and will hold the bond for years. Two-part epoxy comes in two parts (thus the name): a resin and hardener that you mix together when you're ready to use it. Two-minute epoxy dries quickly, which is sometimes a good option for a project. Keep an eye on what you are gluing until you see the glue set. Sometimes parts being glued together will "walk," or slide apart, and adhere in the wrong place if they're not moved back into position. Two-part epoxy is available from a number of different brands.

HOW TO BREAK UP FLAGSTONE, ROCK, OR MARBLE TILE

Wear a face mask and be aware of your surroundings; the shards will fly. Set an opened cardboard box or wood crate on its side on the floor. Bend down in front of it on one knee and hold the tile or flagstone with the toe of your shoe. Using the sledgehammer, firmly tap the chisel against the tile where you want to break it. It will not break up precisely where you're tapping. Breaking up more pieces than you think you'll need will give you more options for fitting pieces together for a patio or path. For stubborn marble and stone that is harder to chisel, use the corner of the sledgehammer directly on the piece and give the tile a hard tap.

OUTDOOR SILICONE GLUE Silicone glue comes in many brands for many different applications for industrial and residential use. For miniature work, choose a high-performance adhesive suitable for outdoors. E6000 is a permanent craft adhesive that works on a variety of materials including wood, metal, resin, and plastic and withstands rain and freezing temperatures. After a few years outdoors, silicone glue will degrade and you will need to clean up and re-glue your miniature.

SUPERGLUE WITH ACCELERATOR An accelerator hardens superglue (cyanoacrylate) instantly. It is usually sold near superglues at craft and hardware stores. You can use this combination two ways, depending on your application: spray the join with the accelerator after you glue the pieces together, or spray the pieces with the accelerator, put them together, then drop the superglue on the join.

ALEENE'S TACKY GLUE Similar to white craft glue, Aleene's Tacky Glue is a lot thicker and holds objects in place while the glue is still wet. It's not waterproof. It's very thick; store it upside down so you don't have to wait for it to pour every time you use it.

HOT GLUE Hot glue is fun to use because it's fast and it sticks but it is seldom weatherproof or waterproof. Save your hot-glue gun sessions for indoor miniatures or for projects that won't be left outdoors during rainy or freezing months. Caveat: be sure to get the right glue for the temperature of your glue-gun. If your glue is always stringy, your gun is not hot enough.

WHITE CRAFT GLUE Basic craft glue is useful to have on hand. It can be used as a light, clear sealer for porous materials to prolong their life, but it is not waterproof.

Mini Patio Mix

To set your patios and pathways properly so that they won't wash away in the rain or when you water overhead, you'll need to set them in a very fine weatherproof grout, such as my original Mini Patio Mix. Other cement-based products, such as exterior mortar mix, or sifted cement, can be used, but Mini Patio Mix is made of superfine sand and delivers a consistent, miniature texture like no other cement-based product can. The texture of exterior mortar is very smooth and not natural; the sifted cement will have irregularities in the size of the sand. Remember that in miniature, it is the tiny details that add up to create the enchantment in a miniature garden.

Use the right glue for the job to make your work last.

Paint

With so many paints available for different purposes, it is easy to clutter up your workbench with bottles, tubes, and cans of paint that you might only use once a year. The following list is an overview of the different kinds of paints that are useful in a miniature garden workshop, but if you have limited space and can choose only one kind, choose a set of high-quality acrylic paints.

ACRYLIC ARTIST PAINT Acrylic artist paint is a pleasure to work with. It comes in a wide variety of colors, cleans up easily with water, is inexpensive, and can be used on wood, resin, plastic, and metal. This type of paint can be watered down to any consistency to suit your purpose. To brush on solid coats of color, add only a couple of drops of water to make the paint more fluid. You can dilute the paint with more water to a milk-like consistency and it will act like a stain. Acrylic paint used straight from the tube or jar is thick and can add texture to the surface of any project, like a faux wood grain or stucco finish. A little goes a long way when you're painting miniatures, so you do not need large quantities of colors to keep in your arsenal.

The difference in quality among acrylic-paint brands can be drastic and often price is not a good indicator of paint quality. Some acrylic artist-paint brands have a rubbery consistency, while others do not cover well and require several coats to get a solid color. If you are trying an unknown brand, test a tube or two before you buy a whole palette. Utrecht acrylic paint is available in vivid colors, goes on smoothly, and covers well. It's made in the USA and can be found in art supply stores and online.

ENAMEL PAINT Enamel model paint is typically used for model boats and airplanes, but is also ideal for miniature garden accessories. It comes in small bottles in all kinds of colors, and is available at hobby shops, art supply stores, and online. It is oil-based, so you'll need turpentine (or equivalent) for cleanup. Enamel paint also comes in an acrylic-base version that is easy to clean up and less smelly.

NAIL POLISH Nail polish is an enamel paint. Use it for customizing miniature garden accessories; it looks

WHAT'S A WASH?

Some of the projects in this book call for applying a wash over the accessory. A wash is simply paint diluted with water, and it supplies a shaded color to the accessory and highlights its textures. Applying more than one wash to an accessory creates subtle layers of color on the piece. For a lighter wash, add more water; for a heavier wash, add less water.

Painting your own accessories with washes of color is a great way to personalize your miniature garden.

Nail polish is an inexpensive enamel paint that works perfectly on accessories for miniature gardens.

especially good on miniature tool handles. Painting your accessories is a great way to use up old bottles of colors that you're no longer wearing. To thin it out, carefully add acetone or nail-polish remover to the bottle of nail polish, a little at a time, then shake the bottle well and test the polish before adding more; you want the polish to have a yogurt-like consistency. Use it on wood, plastic, or metal. If you would like to add sparkle, use glitter nail polish. To protect the strength of the color from fading in sunlight, treat the accessory with a UV-protectant spray once the nail polish has dried, and continue to treat it twice a year to preserve the color.

WOOD STAIN If you want to stain wooden accessories, using real wood stain is ideal. It works well for larger projects, as a little goes a long way in miniature. Wood stain is available in small cans at your local hardware store. Some brands are oil-based (you'll need turpentine to clean them up) and some are water-based for easier cleanup.

LATEX HOUSE PAINT House paint is very useful for painting large surface areas, displays, plant stands, or pots. Latex paints can be easily diluted for washes.

WHAT COLOR IS THAT COLOR?

Burnt Umber = dark chocolate

Cadmium Green = bright light green

Cadmium Yellow Deep = bright orange

Crimson = dark cherry red

Dioxazine Purple = dark navy blue

Magenta = hot pink

Naphthol Red Light = cherry red

Payne's Gray = dark blue-gray

Phthalo Blue = aquamarine blue

Phthalo Green = dark turquoise-blue

Phthalo Yellow Green = lime green

Quicardine = raspberry red

Raw Sienna or **Yellow Oxide** = tan leather

Ultramarine Blue = navy blue

Check your local hardware store for small cans of house paint in a variety of great colors. For some good bargains, look for paints mixed in error.

MINI PAINTBRUSH PRIMER AND CARE

Have you ever wondered what the difference is between all the brushes you see in the art and craft stores? Here's what's what:

- Natural-bristle brushes are for oil-based paint.
- Synthetic-bristle brushes are for acrylic-based paint.

For your miniature garden arsenal, find a variety pack to get started with and pick up a couple of really small brushes for detail work, including one superfine and the smallest, flattest one you can find. Buy a package of cheap disposable paintbrushes as well; these are for discarding after one use.

With proper care, your paintbrushes can last for years. Here are some guidelines for caring for them.

- If paint dries on the brush, use a brush cleaner or restorer to rejuvenate the brush, following the manufacturer's directions.
- Clean your brushes thoroughly after each use. Using a small bowl with a dash of dish soap,

swirl and dab the brush in the bowl; you will see the color come out. Rinse thoroughly under running water. Shake out the excess water and realign the bristles while they're still wet. Let the brush air-dry.

A variety of brushes are handy to have in your arsenal. Use larger paintbrushes to cover large areas, and use fine-tipped brushes for detail work.

SPRAY PAINT Spray paint is ideal for wicker furniture and accessory detailing that might be spoiled with a coat of thick paint. Thankfully, in recent years there have been major advancements in making this kind of paint environmentally friendly. Spray it on in light coats, letting each coat dry before applying another, and avoid a heavy hand so that the paint won't drip or clog the tiny holes in the wicker. Most brands have 2x coverage or similar (meaning one coat of that brand is the same as two coats of another brand), and they come in a fantastic variety of colors.

Be sure to purchase spray paint at a hardware store that has high inventory turnover because old cans that have been sitting unshaken on store shelves tend to stop working when they're half full. Shake the can well before

and during use. Follow the manufacturer's instructions; the newer nozzles do not need to be turned upside down to clean them out after each use.

Hardeners and Stiffeners

Wood hardeners are especially valuable for miniature garden accessories because a lot of the wood that is sold for making models and building model railroads is balsa wood, which is a soft wood that doesn't hold up well in rain and bad weather. Treating balsa and other soft woods with a hardener protects the wood from moisture and strengthens small cuts of wood. Oil-based hardeners are often recommended for tough jobs in the full-size world, but since you're working with small pieces that

Different hardeners for different jobs.

PRESERVING WOOD

Most commercially produced miniature wooden accessories are made of pine or balsa wood. Pine is stronger than balsa wood, but both woods benefit from a wood hardener. You can use wood hardener to make any type of wood stronger, which will help it last longer than it normally would outdoors.

Wood is made of tiny fibers that absorb moisture and expand. The constant movement of the fibers, expanding and contracting, puts stress on glued joints, breaking the chemical bond of the glue and causing the pieces to come apart.

Hardener prevents this from happening by sealing the wood to keep out moisture. Rain or dampness in the air is unable to penetrate sealed wood, preventing it from expanding and contracting in the weather. While the wood will eventually weather, as all things do when left outside, using a hardener extends the life of a wood miniature dramatically.

likely won't cause anyone injuries from structural damage, choose a water-soluble hardener for easy cleanup.

A stiffener is used to weatherproof accessories made of porous materials, such as wood. A popular brand is Mod Podge, which is available in a variety of formulas including one that works as an outdoor sealant. Use light applications of stiffener on accessories that won't get wet often. Paverpol is an industrial-strength textile stiffener that seals any porous material, making it waterproof, and is used in a variety of ways in this book. It is the consistency of glue and can be thinned with water to help it seep into fabric.

Cutting Tools

CRAFT KNIFE A craft knife with a sharp replaceable blade is the handiest knife you will ever use while making miniature accessories. X-Acto Knife No. 11 is a good one to have on hand. Choose one that is comfortable for you to hold and be sure to pick up extra blades.

You may find a cutting mat useful as well. It provides an excellent surface to use with a craft knife. You'll be able to find cutting mats in a variety of sizes at any craft or hardware store.

HANDSAW A handsaw will come in handy, and you can now find smaller options for working with twigs and other wood. Look for a compact hacksaw; it's a one-handled saw with replaceable blades. Blades for many different cutting purposes are available; find one for fine, delicate work and pick up a couple of different types for your arsenal of tools.

MINI MITER SAW Unless you are cutting a lot of pieces, you will only need a miter cut to make angled corners for a door frame or piece of furniture. You can find a

An X-Acto knife, a wood-carving knife, and an old paring knife will all come in handy for your miniature projects.

tabletop miter box set that comes with a saw, but make sure that the box has a place for you to clamp it to your workbench. This is critical for your sanity as it will save you from trying to hold everything together with one hand and saw with the other.

Carving tips and safety precautions

ALWAYS BE AWARE OF THE LINE OF CUT. This is the direction the knife will go as you cut. This is the most important rule for working with anything sharp, including power tools. The line of cut extends beyond the material you're cutting to include the possibility of the knife slipping. For example, if you're carving toward your body and the knife slides a little too quickly, you run the risk of stabbing yourself. Instead of risking a trip to the hospital, always carve in a direction away from your body.

When you're carving miniatures, be especially vigilant: notice how you're holding the piece and keep your fingers and arms away from the line of cut. With practice this will become second nature.

ALWAYS USE A SHARP KNIFE. Dull knives drag and can cause unnecessary slipping. A sharp blade is a pleasure to use and puts less stress on your hands and wrists.

HOLD THE PIECE YOU'RE CARVING GENTLY. Remember, it's miniature. Be careful not to apply too much pressure, and carve it in small passes rather than trying to carve off a big chunk of wood at once.

CARVE IN THE DIRECTION OF THE WOOD GRAIN. Keep in mind that wood is made of fibers that run parallel to each other. If you are having difficulty carving, you may be carving against the grain.

Creating a spot to make miniature gardens can be just as creative as making the gardens.

WORLD TOUR

AMERICA

Cape Cod is one of America's most iconic and recognizable regions. It was a landmark for early explorers and an anchorage point for pilgrims arriving in the New World. Cape Cod's long, windy beaches, grassy knolls, picket fences, and lapping waves conjure peaceful images. Here you can imagine sitting back, relaxing, and watching the world go by. What a perfect theme for a miniature garden. Or perhaps it should be called a miniature vacation?

The accessories that make up a Cape Cod theme can easily be adapted to other beach locales, even international ones. By simply painting the Adirondack chair a bright flamingo pink and planting small-leafed sedums and succulents, you can move the beach to seaside Florida. A pale lemon–colored chair paired with a light turquoise pot or two can evoke a beach in the south of France.

If you want water in your garden, consider a natural solution, rather than a store-bought pond. You can hint at the idea of water by making part of the garden slope down to a sandy area sprinkled with driftwood and tiny shells. Or use a piece of heavy black plastic and build a pond in the soil. Adhere the plastic to the side of the pot with silicone glue to make the shore deeper than ground level so the water will collect there. Simpler solutions are using a black frozen-food container as a pond liner and

A variegated cotoneaster provides a bit of shade.

hiding the edges with stones, or using a smaller pot as an in-ground pool.

In this set of projects you will learn how to harden and seal different porous materials for outdoor use, explore a way to age wood furniture in a few simple steps, and make a hanging planter from a snail shell.

Planting Cape Cod

To replicate a beach scene in a miniature garden, try mugo pines for their rugged appearance and ground-cover junipers nestled with stringy dwarf lily turf, a grassy looking plant evocative of windswept dunes. Use taller trees to anchor the bed. Look for small-leafed shrubs like young, variegated cotoneaster with a broad canopy to fit a chair underneath. Place miniature driftwood logs randomly to give the impression the tide washed them ashore, or use them to line a path to a deck where a weathered Adirondack chair invites you to sit for a spell.

How to Age Wood Miniatures

BY CREATING NICKS AND WORN SPOTS By beating up an accessory to give it nicks and worn spots, you can add decades to new wooden chairs, decks, or trellises. Find miniature wood accessories at your local craft or dollar store; they're unfinished and are usually made of pine or balsa wood.

Use details sparingly, so that
you don't overload the scene.

The process of beating up miniature wooden accessories was inspired by techniques for aging full-size furniture. Creating a shabby chic or antique appearance can be accomplished using several techniques, including denting the wood by whipping it with chains, making haphazard scrapes and grooves by placing the piece on gravel and stepping on it, softening edges by sanding them down, or making slashes and grooves using a knife (or a combination of approaches). These are similar to methods used on full-size furniture, but they're applied with a much lighter touch because you are working with small pieces.

BY APPLYING LAYERS OF PAINT At first glance, a weathered piece of wood furniture might look gray. But if you look closely at any naturally aged wood, you will see many colors, not just gray. Tan-colored sections, dark brown spots, or lighter brown streaks appear on the wood and mingle with blue-grays and silver sheens. Red or mahogany hues may run through the wood's pattern, or you might see green mossy spots if the wood lives in a damper climate.

You can emulate nature's palette and age unfinished wood furniture by painting it in layers of color. Using brighter washes of color before applying a final wash of Payne's gray will add depth to the wood, simulating age and weathering.

Make something new look old. This Adirondack chair was made to look weathered using washes of paint and techniques for beating up the wood.

PROJECT
AGING ADIRONDACKS

The first step for weathering and aging a wood Adirondack chair is to focus on the parts of the chair that get used the most, such as the feet, seat, and armrests. These parts get the most wear and tear, so extra attention should be spent on them to make them look worn.

TOOLS AND MATERIALS

Wood Adirondack chair

Sharp knife

Sandpaper, rough and fine grit

Emery board

Clean, soft rag

Small can or jar

Wood hardener

Paintbrushes, one disposable, one small

Acrylic paint in light green, magenta, Payne's gray, and white

Paint tray

UV-protectant spray

↑ Layers of color, instead of a single coat of gray, create depth and age on this chair.

1 Using the carving knife, shave off all the corners of each board on the chair. Carve off the edges a little at a time, taking more material off the main areas of the chair, the ends of the armrests, and the lower part of the legs. Work your way around the chair until all the edges have been carved.

2 Using the rough sandpaper, sand each edge until it's smooth, working around the chair methodically so you don't miss an edge. Fold the sandpaper to get it into the tighter spaces. Using the fine sandpaper, do another round of sanding. Soften and round off each edge of each board on the chair.

3 Use the emery board to sand in between the slats. Wipe off the dust with the dry cloth.

4 Using the carving knife, carefully score the tops of the armrests in random spots, the seat, and the back of the chair. Score the legs of the chair, too.

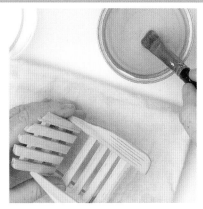

5 Pour a small amount of hardener into the can. Using the disposable paintbrush, apply hardener to all the sides of each board of the chair. Work methodically to cover each side of each board; the hardener will protect the wood against water and give it a longer life. Let dry for as long as the hardener manufacturer recommends.

6 Mix a small amount of magenta paint with water to make a wash. Using the small paintbrush, blot the paint sporadically on all sides of the chair. Dab off any excess paint with the cloth. Repeat this step using a wash of light green. Let dry.

7 With the Payne's gray paint, mix a thicker stain, like the consistency of cream, and paint a wash on one area of the chair at a time. If you try to paint all sides at once, the paint will dry and you will not be able to get the pink and green colors to show through. Paint in between the slats and be sure all sides of the slats are painted. Dab off any excess paint with the cloth and keep dabbing the paint off until you like the appearance of the chair. Let dry.

8 Start this next step on the underside of the chair so you can get the hang of it before you work on the top side. Use undiluted white paint to whitewash over the gray color. Spackle, brush, or dab (or use all three techniques) the white paint on with a paintbrush. Smudge the brushstrokes with a finger. Use the cloth to dab off any excess paint if needed. Let the paint dry for at least an hour, then spray the chair with UV-protectant spray.

SNAIL SHELL PLANTER

Snail shells make charming planters for miniature gardens. Make sure the shell you choose is a large one; large shells are the hardest and most developed and can withstand having holes drilled in them. Shells about 1 inch long are the perfect size for a large-scale (1-inch scale) miniature garden, and they can easily accommodate a couple of sedum cuttings. Young snails have very brittle shells that crush from the lightest pressure. A mature snail shell is usually more than 1 inch long. The perfect time to go snail hunting in the garden is after it rains, but the simplest way is to let them come to you by using a beer trap or slug bait.

You may be able to find larger snail shells, but keep in mind the scale of your garden and imagine a full-size hanging snail planter; it would be about one foot in length.

There are several ways to extract a living snail from its shell, but the least disgusting method is to let the snail dry up inside its shell and leave it there so that you don't have to touch it. The snail may take a day or a week to dry up, depending on how hot and dry the weather is. Eventually the snail's body will biodegrade. Occasionally, the dried carcass will dislodge while you're drilling holes in the shell and you'll be able to pull it out with your fingers or tweezers.

This project requires a light touch. Even though you're working with a mature shell and using hardener to stiffen the shell, it is still delicate. When you're threading the wire through the holes and winding the wire around itself to fasten it, don't use the shell as leverage to bend the wire. If you push on the shell with the wire, the shell will break. Instead, push, bend, and pinch the wire using only the other end of the wire as leverage. Collect more than one shell in case you break it on your first attempt.

The hardener used in this project is wood hardener, but you can use clear or colored enamel nail polish instead if you like. The wire used in this project is 28 gauge (a great size for most miniature garden projects and purposes). The shell is really lightweight and does not require much to support it even when it's planted.

← Made from a snail shell, this whimsical planter holds small sedum cuttings.

↓ The snails will dry up by themselves with a little help from slug bait.

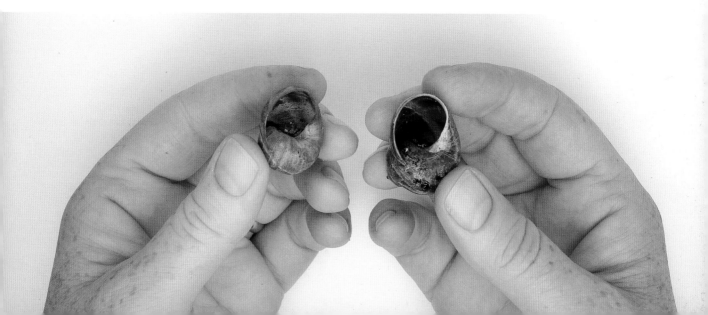

INSTRUCTIONS

TOOLS AND MATERIALS

Snail shell, about 1 inch long

Paintbrush

Wood hardener or enamel nail polish

Small drill with ¹⁄₁₆-inch bit

28-gauge floral wire, 8 inches

Round-nose pliers

Flat-nose pliers

1 Holding the shell gently, use the paintbrush to apply hardener on the shell. Let dry.

2 Holding the snail shell gently but firmly, with the opening facing up, drill one hole on each side of the shell, where the shell is a single layer, so you can draw the wire through the holes easily.

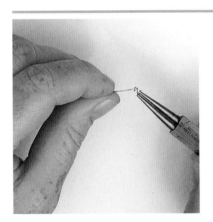

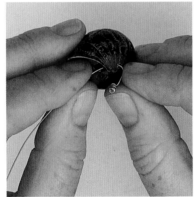

3 Using the round-nose pliers, curl one end of the wire tightly to make it look like a small tendril on a vine.

4 From the outside of the shell, thread the uncurled end of the wire into one of the holes and pull it through to just about the curled part. Bend the wire into a U-shape, making sure not to push against the shell. Press against the wire by holding the wire, not the shell.

5 Loop the tendril around the wire close to the edge of the shell to fasten it loosely onto the shell. Do not make a tightly fitted loop because it may break the shell.

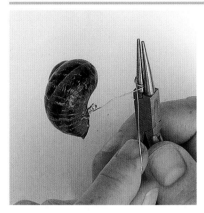 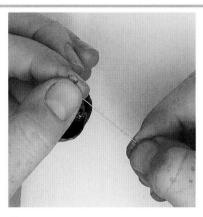 

6 About 1 inch up from where the wires are looped around each other, where the wire is U-shaped, make one or two loops around the round-nose pliers to make a ring for hanging the planter.

7 If the wire gets bent in the process, run your fingers along the wire to straighten it. You can also use the flat-nose pliers to iron out any bends or bumps in the wire.

8 Carefully thread the other end of the wire (the uncurled end) through the other hole in the shell and pull it through gently, holding the wire to avoid putting any pressure on the shell.

9 Bend the uncurled end of the wire around itself to fasten it, and use the flat-nose pliers to gently press the two wires together. Twirl the end of the wire around the round-nose pliers to make another small tendril. Straighten the wire hanger and even out the loop so the planter hangs evenly, and again be careful not to use the shell as leverage. Go get some sedum cuttings to plant, and admire your handiwork.

Hang the snail
shell planter off
to the side and
out of the way of
the chair.

GREAT BRITAIN

With its history and literature, charming villages and magnificent gardens, Great Britain casts a spell over the imagination. London, a world capital renowned for its landmarks, is home to such grand open spaces as Hyde Park and St. James's Park and also teems with gardens large and small, as well as pocket parks and alcoves of greenery throughout the city and along the River Thames. A miniature garden is the perfect stage for a British park scene.

When you consider the countless elements that can illustrate English life, it's difficult to narrow them down to just a few for your garden. Avoid obvious British icons like the Tower of London or the Union Jack, and try to evoke the *feeling* of Britain instead. Britain's cities and villages are old, so think about how you can represent that age in a miniature garden. For example, use accessories made of materials that have been used in gardens for centuries, like terra-cotta, stone, wood, and metal.

To accessorize your garden, think of typical garden accents that can be viewed as quintessentially British.

A park bench in a charming English garden is a lovely place to sit for a spell.

For example, miniature streetlamps are available in many different styles, so, using the Internet as a guide, find an English-style streetlamp. Choose garden statuary that is typical of the region. A fox or hound statue, a knight in armor, or Britain's national animal, the Barbary lion (make sure it is a *Chronicles of Narnia*–type lion, a friendly-looking male with a huge mane), will all lend a British aura to a garden. A bust or statue of a member of the royal family, or an English poet, writer, or musician will work as well. A miniature statue of Charles Dickens suited the theme of this garden to a tee.

The other accents chosen to deliver the theme here are an aged park bench, typical of the benches you see throughout London, a brown paper bag with spilled bird-seed, and an opportunistic squirrel. There's another brown paper bag that has been blown about too, underneath the bench, as a public park would typically have a bit of trash somewhere. This starts the storytelling. Notice that it's the little messes, or the evidence that someone has just been here, that pique interest and invite the question, "What is going on here?"

The two projects that follow work as important scene setters, giving the park a well-established atmosphere and a backdrop for the other details: a brick patio or path, aged to look as if it has seen a lot of history, and a folly, also crafted to look old, with plants all around to give the impression that they're starting to overtake the structure.

Planting Great Britain

When choosing plants for this project, look for a tree that appears old. Park trees are often unkempt and not well maintained, so a carefully manicured tree wouldn't look as if it had been around for a while. With its branches splaying outward, this 'Jacqueline Verkade' dwarf Canada hemlock has a perfect canopy, and with its nice trunk and branching system it looks like a well-established tree, making it perfect for a park scene. The tree is taller than the folly, with enough room to tuck a tiny cypress shrub underneath it to add additional interest to the garden bed.

The groundcovers were chosen for their colors as well as their compatibility with the other plants in the container. The brown leaves of 'Platt's Black' brass buttons match the brown pot, bricks, and bench. The blades of the dwarf mondo grass add a contrast in texture to the tiny daisies behind the park bench to create a garden for full, cool sun, and regular watering.

↑Even miniature squirrels can't resist the opportunity to stop and enjoy the park bench. Details such as birdseed spilling out of a paper bag add another layer to the scene.

→'Jacqueline Verkade' dwarf Canada hemlock stands tall in this wee park.

PROJECT
ANCIENT BRICK PATIO

To create a well-worn brick path or patio, age a sheet of large dollhouse bricks. The choice between brick or stone for this project was straightforward: it is much easier to make new terra-cotta bricks look weathered than it is to make stones look weathered.

With a couple of bashing techniques and some layers of paint, you can give the bricks an ancient feel. Included in the materials list are two colors for the final washes, burnt umber and Payne's gray, which add age, but you can skip using the gray if you like. Burnt umber matched the garden container perfectly, so that color is all this patio needed for its final wash. Payne's gray will make a darker patio that would suit a gray or blue pot nicely.

TOOLS AND MATERIALS

One or two sheets of high-fired terra-cotta bricks, or enough to cover the patio area in your garden

Sanding blocks, large and small

Acrylic paint in light green, dark green, burnt umber, and Payne's gray

Paintbrush, medium size

Clean, soft rag

↑ This age-old brick could be a well-worn path or a patio that has seen all kinds of weather.

INSTRUCTIONS

1 Expose the bricks' edges by folding the sheet over the edge of a table so that the long sides of the bricks are parallel with the table's edge. Working on one row at a time, run the large sanding block gently over the edges and corners of the bricks, but be somewhat random so that the weathering appears natural. If any bricks fall off, put them aside to glue on later.

2 Turn the sheet 90 degrees, fold the sheet over the edge of the table, and sand the short sides of the bricks with the large sanding block. Make sure all the sharp edges and corners have been softened on each brick. Use the smaller sanding block to sand down any areas the large sanding block can't reach.

3 Mix a small amount of light green paint with water until the mixture has the consistency of cream. Using a paintbrush, dot the brick sheet randomly with the green paint.

4 Use the rag to blot off any excess paint and help soften the edges of the color. Let dry.

5 Repeat steps 3 and 4 using dark green paint. Let dry.

6 Mix a small amount of burnt umber with water until the mixture has the consistency of cream. Paint the sheet with the burnt umber wash. If necessary, bend the sheet of bricks in order to apply paint onto the sides of each brick.

7 Use a rag to wipe off any excess burnt umber paint.

8 Gradually cover the entire sheet of bricks with light washes of burnt umber paint. Let dry. If you would like a deeper color, apply more paint and let dry.

9 Once the paint is dry, the weathered brick patio is ready to install in your miniature garden.

PROJECT
A FOLLY IN THE PARK

A folly imparts some history into your miniature park. You start with a cut stone or a brick that has several flat sides, for the foundation. The stone makes the folly heavy, which allows the folly to stand up in the soil without any support. You can use another type of material for the folly's foundation, but be sure that it's a material that isn't porous. For example, wood will not work as a foundation because it expands and contracts with moisture, and any stones that you try to adhere to it will not remain glued on.

The stones used in this project are from a sheet of stone tiles, available at hardware stores or miniature garden shops. You can use loose stones instead, gluing them on individually and letting the glue dry completely before moving on to the next side of the foundation (so that you don't dislodge the stones while the glue is still wet). Make sure all stones are dry before you begin gluing them to the rock, so that they adhere properly.

↑ This stone folly has an aura of decay, giving the impression it's been in this garden for centuries.

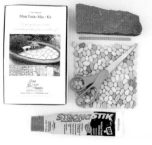

TOOLS AND MATERIALS

Stone sheet with enough stones to cover the foundation

Foundation rock or a small brick

Scissors

Heavy-duty exterior adhesive

Popsicle stick for spreading glue

Box cutter

Mini Patio Mix, ½ pound

Gloves

Bowl

Spoon

Sponge

Large plastic bag

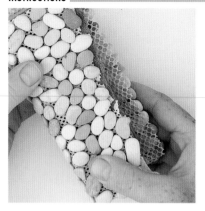

1 Wrap the stone sheet around three sides of the rock so that you can gauge how it fits and where to glue it to the rock. You will cut off any excess once you're done and the adhesive has dried completely.

2 Apply the adhesive onto one side of the rock and use the popsicle stick to spread it out. (Be sure to read the glue manufacturer's directions; some adhesives require a wait time before joining.)

3 Line up the bottom edge of the sheet of stones with the bottom edge of the rock and press the sheet of stones onto the side of the rock into the glue. Press the sheet firmly to the rock to make sure all the stones make contact with the glue.

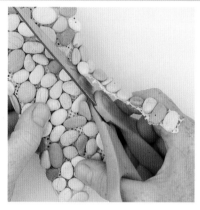

4 Repeat steps 2 and 3 for the two other sides of the rock, pressing the sheet of stones to each side firmly before proceeding to the next side. Be sure that you've covered as much of the rock's surface as possible, but leave the top, bottom, and one side of the rock uncovered to make it look old and deteriorated. Let the adhesive dry for as long as the manufacturer recommends.

5 Once the adhesive is completely dry, use scissors or a box cutter to cut off any excess stones from around the edges of the rock. Cut off any parts of the mesh that may be hanging off or sticking up, too.

6 In a bowl, prepare a small batch of Mini Patio Mix by slowly adding water to the mix, a little at a time, and stir with a spoon until the mix is the consistency of cookie dough.

7 Wearing gloves and working on one side of the folly at a time, press the wet Mini Patio Mix in between the stones. Be meticulous about pressing the mix in between the stones, and double-check to see that all the nooks and crannies are filled before moving on to the next step.

8 Dampen a sponge with water and gently clean off the surface of the stones. Rinse the sponge and repeat on all sides. Make sure all the seams and any exposed mesh are covered with the mix.

9 Place the folly in a plastic bag and sprinkle a few drops of water in the bag before you close it. Wait three to five days before removing the folly from the bag. The longer the mix has to dry the stronger it will be. Position the folly toward the back of the garden, tucked in among the plants so that it looks like foliage has grown up around it. Call your local historical society to tell them about the ancient piece of architecture you found in your garden.

GARDEN FOLLY

A folly is a small decorative building that serves no function except to create a picturesque effect. The word folly comes from the French folie, meaning madness or silliness. Follies were very popular in eighteenth-century French and English gardens, deliberately built as ornaments and often resembling small castles, towers, temples, villages, mills, or any type or part of a building, usually constructed to appear already ruined in order to allude to a bygone era. Some follies were made in the shape of a Chinese temple or Tartar tent in a tribute to exotic lands. Today, follies are still used in garden design, in the same spirit of whimsy that originally inspired them.

In a miniature garden design, you can add a folly to evoke age and permanence in the garden bed. A folly will also help stage the scene by creating a backdrop against which to plant your garden, like a backdrop in a theatre. A backdrop element in your miniature garden will keep the viewer's eye focused on the design of the garden.

A seemingly ancient piece of architecture anchors this picturesque garden.

SPAIN

Spain is a country rich in creativity, as seen in the music, food, art, and architecture. So it is not surprising to find a wonderfully distinct garden style, too. Spain has had many layers of influence on its culture because of its history and geographical position on Europe's Iberian peninsula. You can see Moorish, Mediterranean, and Northern European influences in the gardens. Some of Spain's most popular gardens are huge estates full of rows of carefully manicured cypress trees separating different areas where you will find Moorish-style buildings mixed with Italian-style hedges and English-style boxwood hedges lining Roman-style baths and adorned with Italian statues.

When you consider the colors of Spain, its distinctive architecture, and its epic landscapes, as well as the personality of the people, there is an exciting palette of inspiration to choose from. The applied arts of pottery and mosaics burst with color, illustrating Spain's flora in richly colored tints and tones. You can bring that excitement of color into your miniature Spanish garden with pots, furniture, garden art, and a patio or pathway. Don't be afraid of mixing together bright colors like cobalt blue, pumpkin orange, or bright yellow.

Small Spanish gardens are very cozy and inviting. If the garden is not a courtyard, it is usually sheltered somehow with at least one wall on one side to provide

A perfect place to dance to the music of flamenco.

shade from the hot sun. Small trees supply additional shade and add an air of softness to the hard wall or walls. Because of the hot and arid Spanish climate, water features are popular in Spanish gardens; it's not unusual to find a sizable water fountain in a small Spanish garden. This type of garden often has a cafe-style table and chairs for enjoying a café con leche or tapas, so include a place to sit down to eat in your miniature garden.

Planting Spain

When thinking about plants that would convey a Spanish atmosphere, take a moment to consider Spain's Mediterranean climate. Because of the heat, the plants you see in the Spanish landscape are rugged and sturdy enough to survive the country's hot sun and dry air. For this project a leggy 'Tequila Sunrise' coprosma is the perfect candidate for a small patio tree, not only for its weathered look but for its size and the color of its leaves as well. Other suggestions for small patio trees are very young, evergreen slow-growing shrubs like English boxwood, any Japanese euonymus, and dwarf elms like 'Seiju' or 'Jacqueline Hillier' for larger pots. The bedding plants, dwarf mondo grass, and green carpet (*Herniaria glabra*) were chosen for their crisp texture and matching color. Other miniature but rugged choices are red thyme, *Scleranthus biflorus* (sometimes called Australian AstroTurf), and sea thrift (*Armeria maritima*).

There is always a place to sit and savor a café con leche.

A leggy coprosma helps deliver shade.

For more ideas for nationally themed gardens, consider these items that represent a country:

- Flag colors
- National animal or bird
- National traditions

- National culinary dishes
- Colors of the nation's major sports teams
- National monuments

The bull is Spain's national animal.

PROJECT
AGING A FOUNTAIN

Can't find an accessory in the right color for your garden? Paint it! Take a close look at any old stone or concrete and you will see many layers of colors, swaths of green moss, and, on stone, areas where mildew has made the stone a deeper shade of brown. On a fountain, you might see dark green blemishes around the outside of the basin or at the fountain's base near the ground. On top of the fountain, or on any side that faces the sun, there may be areas where the color has faded completely. Old, weathered stone has many colors on it. If you try to age a piece by painting it standard gray, made up of white and black paint, the result will appear flat and one-dimensional. It takes layers of color to convey aged stone.

With a few washes of acrylic paint, you can mimic Mother Nature's palette and transform a new accessory into an aged accessory. In this project, you will learn how to use layers of paint to age a plain resin fountain, starting with a layer of pink paint. By using pink for the first layer, you create a new base color to build on. When the washes that follow are added to the top of the pink wash, they create deeper patches of color on the fountain, giving it the weathered appearance of a mottled stone fountain.

For a different result, use a different color for the final layer. For example, a wash of Payne's gray will give the fountain a stone gray appearance, but a richer, bluer, and more interesting gray than the original color, which pairs nicely with granite or charcoal-colored flagstone. Or a final wash of burnt umber will create a deep earthy look of chiseled stone.

Layer washes of color to create age.

TOOLS AND MATERIALS

Acrylic paint in cadmium green, magenta, raw sienna, brilliant blue

Paintbrush, medium size

Resin fountain

Clean, soft rag

UV-protectant spray

INSTRUCTIONS

1 Mix a small amount of magenta paint with water until the mixture is the consistency of milk. Test the strength of the color on the back or bottom of the fountain to make sure the color is the saturation you desire. Using the paintbrush, randomly dab the wash all over the front of the fountain.

2 Using the rag, dab off the excess and blend the pink wash into the color of the fountain. To make the color stronger, add another layer of wash. Let dry.

3 Repeat step 1, but use the green paint. Make a wash, dab it on randomly, and use a rag to soften the brushstrokes with the magenta wash. Make sure you dab paint around the base, around the basin (but not inside the basin), and where the imaginary sun wouldn't shine; that's where moss would grow. Let dry.

4 Mix a thicker wash using raw sienna and test the intensity of the color on the back side of the fountain. Adjust the water-to-paint ratio if you need to. Mottle the wash on one section of the fountain at a time by dabbing the paint on with the brush while it's still wet. Dab off the excess using a rag. Repeat until all the surface areas are covered. Take care not to paint inside the basins or on the resin stream of water. Let dry.

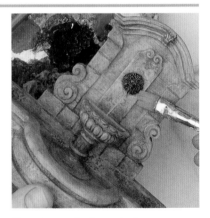

5 Look over the fountain for any spots you may have missed. Add an additional layer of color to the underside of the top basin and to the bottom corners and edges of the fountain to give it more drama.

6 Mix a small amount of blue paint with water to make a wash. Using a paintbrush, carefully paint both basins to give them the appearance of having water in them. Let dry, then spray the fountain with UV-protectant spray. Spray the fountain twice a year with UV-protectant spray to hold the color.

Washes of pink, green, and yellow give the fountain an aged, weathered appearance.

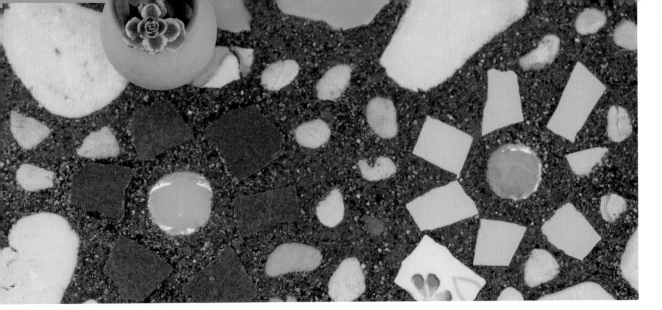

PROJECT
PRETTY MOSAIC PATIO

Patios can be made from a variety of materials, such as tile, stone, or brick. Colorful terra-cotta tiles are a popular accent found in Spanish gardens; you'll see them placed strategically among the tilework on walls and fountains or used as tabletops. The colors of the terra-cotta tiles often reflect Spain's favorite color palette: cobalt blue, pumpkin orange, and sunny yellow. In this project we are going to create a mosaic patio using a variety of materials, including tile, glass marbles, and stone.

Find tile pieces for your mosaic patio by canvasing thrift stores and second-use building-supply stores. Look for broken and chipped dishes in colors and patterns that will match your design. Ignore the overall pattern of the plate, platter, or bowl and focus instead on its colors because once the dish is broken into tiny pieces the pattern won't be visible.

TOOLS AND MATERIALS

Planted miniature garden, with an area cleared for a border and patio

Sand, ¼ pound

Border material, such as wood

Sheet of paper

Pencil

Mosaic materials, including assorted pieces of glass and tile, and marbles

Tile clippers

Safety glasses

Mini Patio Mix, ½ pound

Spoon

Bowl

Skewer

Small wood block

Mister

↑ **Combine tile and rock in a patio for more interest.**

HOW TO CUT TILE

To shape the tile pieces to make a tighter patio pattern, cut the tiles with tile clippers. Here are some points to consider:

1. Cutting tile is easier than you might imagine.

2. Get a small pair of tile clippers with a comfortable handle that fits easily in your hand. If you're going to do a lot of snipping, it will be easier with a tile clipper that fits your hand well.

3. Wear safety glasses; they'll deflect any shards that fly off the tiles toward your eyes.

4. Snip the tiles over a box to corral the majority of the shards.

5. Snip off a tiny piece at a time. If you try to snip off too much at once, the tile may crack.

6. Instead of cutting a tile to make a tiny adjustment, sand the edges instead. Do not sand the surface of the tile because the sandpaper will scratch the finish.

7. Different kinds of china and pottery react to clipping in different ways. Earthenware is softer than porcelain and will break in a straighter line, for example. Use a few pieces of tile as test pieces to become familiar with how the material breaks before you begin cutting tiles for your final design.

INSTRUCTIONS

1 Install a border around the patio area in your planted garden. Make the patio area 1 inch deep and level it out. Cover the patio area with a layer of sand about ¼ inch deep. Determine where you would like to position the fountain so that you can plan the patio tiles around it.

2 Lay the sheet of paper on top of the patio area and use a pencil to trace an outline of the patio area. As you trace the patio area, check under the paper if you need to in order to make the outline as accurate as possible. Be sure to include the area where the fountain will be if your fountain is sitting on top of the patio.

3 Place the sheet of paper on a work surface and begin designing the patio mosaic. Arrange the tiles, marbles, and stone fragments until you have a composition you like. If you need to, trim the tiles to make them fit better. (See the sidebar on how to cut the tiles.)

4 Using a spoon, gently spread a layer of Mini Patio Mix at least ½ inch deep over the sand.

5 Lay the tiles for the major parts of the design in first; for this patio the tile flowers were placed first. Use a skewer to help adjust the pieces as you work. Fill in the area in between the flower pieces with a neutral-colored stone or tile to help highlight the pattern and colors.

6 When your mosaic is in place, use a wood block or large piece of tile to tamp down the tiles and make the patio surface level.

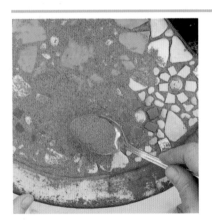

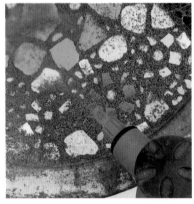

7 Using a spoon, carefully fill the spaces between the tiles with more Mini Patio Mix. If you knock a tile out of place, use the skewer to nudge it back. With the side of your hand, gently brush off the excess Mini Patio Mix and collect it for another use.

8 Activate the Mini Patio Mix by gently misting the patio, and clean the cement residue off the top of the tiles at the same time. When water starts to pool on the surface, stop misting. Let the patio dry for a few hours before touching it. It's now time for a siesta.

Choose miniature furniture with colors that match or complement the rest of the colors in the garden.

INDIA

India is abundant with history, architecture, and arts, making its culture complex and visually stimulating, even in how it worships. The sights, sounds, smells, and colors of India brim with inspiration for a miniature garden. With so much to draw from, the challenge is where to start and what to honor.

When you are starting with absolutely nothing but an urge to make an India-themed miniature garden, you need to find a way to begin. Consider the purpose of the garden: do you want a spot to relax in? How would you envision that in India? Do you want a personal altar at which to meditate? An altar accented with two colorful parasols to bring a touch of India's colors to the scene is the theme of this garden.

Planting India

Now that you have a focal point, consider the garden that will surround the altar. India, the seventh-largest country in the world, has a dynamic geography. With the lofty mountains of the Himalayas, the vast, arid Thar Desert, many rain forests, and hundreds of islands in the Bay of Bengal, the options for planting an India-themed garden are indeed limitless. But it is the lush, tropical rain

A meditation altar perfectly suited
for an India-themed garden.

forests that come to mind as a portion of India that can be condensed into a pot.

Characteristics of a rain forest are dense plantings, heavy textures, and green, green, and more green. Choose plants that look tropical, lush, and exotic and will thrive in the light and temperature levels your garden will receive. Big leaves, tall trees with expansive canopies, thick underbrush, and spikes of unusual foliage will make your garden look like a tropical oasis.

This is where you can use young, faster growing plants. Build a miniature rain forest using the three layers that Mother Nature uses in her work: the top tier is the taller tree canopy that will get the most light; the middle layer is small trees; and the lowest, bottom layer is the dense forest floor where the altar would be. For example, in this garden, the stand of young Norfolk pines are the upper tier, ferns make up the middle layer, and baby tears and small houseplants make up the ground level. The ferns are still in their pots to help keep the moisture around their roots; otherwise the moisture would be wicked away in the large bowl of soil.

Young spider plants were used in the middle of the jungle to add more drama, supplied by their variegated foliage. Plant these types of plants knowing that they will outgrow the spot in one growing season, so leave them in their pots, too. Behind the altar is a sugar vine with big palm-like leaves.

Water Features

Another element that works well in a rain-forest garden is a water feature. Adding a water feature to a miniature garden brings a touch of realism that is inexpensive to achieve, and it requires care, giving you an opportunity to play around in the garden occasionally. Standing water anywhere tends to get a bit stinky, but because miniature garden water features are so small, it will be months before the water feature needs tending to. Maintaining the water feature is easy: simply remove the pond from the garden, being careful not to disturb any soil, clean it out, and replace it gently, tucking it underneath any hanging foliage. You'll be able to find different containers and vessels for a miniature pond at a thrift store. The pond used in this project used to be the bottom dish for a tabletop fountain.

A miniature rain forest.

A little flower floats in the pond.

PROJECT
MEDITATION ALTAR

This altar is meant to be personal, so design it in a way that pleases you, but be sure to make it large enough to hold the figure you've chosen. Have the figure on hand, or at least know how tall it is, while you're making the altar so you can check the fit. Find the stone tiles at your local hardware store in the tile or flooring section; they'll have a range of colors, sizes, and shapes. The sheets come either in strips meant for a backsplash or in 12 × 12-inch squares for flooring. The stone tiles are glued to a mesh sheet and are easy to peel off, but be sure to wear gloves when you're peeling off the stones because the mesh is made of fiberglass. Don't worry if the color of the tiles isn't exactly the same color as the altar; you will be applying a wash of paint over the altar when you are done, which will bring the colors together nicely.

Ganesha sits on the altar in this garden, with vases of flowers on either side and parasols placed for shade. Traditional Indian protocol would insist on the parasols being used to shelter the idol and the plates of tangerines and candles. However, this is your own personal altar to design as you wish.

TOOLS AND MATERIALS

A sheet of tiles or a border pattern

Variety of stone tiles: 1 × 1 inch, 2 × 2 inches, 2 × 4 inches, and 4 × 4 inches

One or more figures or icons

Silicone glue

Acrylic paint in burnt umber

Paintbrush

Clean, soft rag

↑ **Leave room on the altar to display some flowers and candles in addition to the figure you've selected as the focal point.**

1 Peel off a selection of stone tiles from the sheets. Use scissors to trim off the glue around the edges if it shows.

2 Arrange and rearrange the stone tiles to see how you might fit them together. Use the larger stone tiles to create a base first, then reposition the remaining stone tiles until you have a construction that will feature your figure in a way that you like. Measure the figure against the altar and adjust the altar's size if necessary.

3 Take apart the stone tiles (if you think you might forget how the tiles were arranged, make a sketch or snap a photo of the altar before taking it apart) and, beginning with the base, start gluing the stone tiles together. Glue the tiles for the back of the altar together separately from the base to make it easier to work with. Let the glue dry completely after you've glued each section before moving on to the next part.

4 Glue on the smaller decorative stone tiles. Paint the altar with a wash of burnt umber and dab it with a clean, dry rag to get rid of the excess paint. Let dry.

5 The final wash of burnt umber acrylic paint blends all the different colored stone tiles together. Install in the garden and queue the meditation music.

PROJECT
AN INDIAN PARASOL

To infuse the brilliant colors of India into a miniature garden use a colorful container, plant brightly colored foliage, position vibrantly hued objects of devotion on the altar, or bring in another recognizably Indian accessory. In this project, colorful parasols lend bright colors to the garden. Indian parasols are absolutely gorgeous and sometimes feature hand-stitched embroidery, enhancing their beauty. Here, you'll make a simplified version of an Indian parasol, but one that's just as colorful.

You will need several cocktail umbrellas. Acquire them by ordering a few mai tais in the Bahamas, or buy a pack of them in any store with a party section.

An ornate parasol simplified for miniature.

TOOLS AND MATERIALS

Cocktail umbrellas

Paverpol

Flat-nose pliers

Nylon paintbrush, small

Lace ribbon, a little longer than the
   diameter of the parasol

Acrylic paint in one or two colors

Paint tray

1 Open an umbrella and push the small rubber band up to keep the umbrella from closing. Using the paintbrush, paint the entire umbrella, exterior and interior and including the stick, with a thick and thorough coat of Paverpol. Let dry.

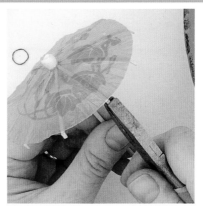

2 Use the flat-nose pliers to bend the tips (the part that extends beyond the paper) of the parasol's cardboard spokes to a 90-degree angle at the edge of the parasol. You will feel the spokes snap; don't pull on them.

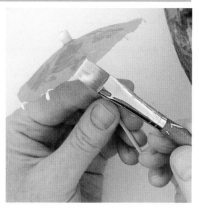

3 Using the flat side of the paintbrush, place a dollop of Paverpol on each bent spoke. The bent spokes will support the ribbon after it's wrapped around them.

4 Brush a generous coat of Paverpol on both sides of the ribbon. Wrap the ribbon around the parasol on the bent spokes, pressing the ribbon gently against the spokes so that it adheres to them. Overlap the end of the ribbon slightly when you reach your starting point.

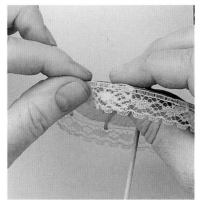

5 Adjust the bent spokes if necessary so that they are perpendicular to the parasol, and straighten the ribbon. Let dry.

6 Paint the parasol, exterior and interior and including the stick, any combination of bright colors. Let dry, then apply another coat of Paverpol all over the parasol. Let dry. Place them in your garden and bring the picnic basket.

JAPAN

BACK TO BASICS

If you are stuck and can't figure out what the next step is, or why your idea isn't working, return to the basic elements of garden design: balance, form, texture, shape, pattern, repetition, and color. Then you'll be able to diagnose the problem, add to or subtract from the design, or change something else to make it work.

Japanse garden design is synonymous with peacefulness. The size of the garden doesn't matter; it can be acres or inches across and it will still convey a sense of serenity and relaxation. A Japanese garden urges you to take a deep breath and just be in the moment. Here's a miniature garden idea that will deliver that magic.

Use the same design principles as you would for any other type of garden. When you're considering all the elements of your composition, take into account balance, texture, shape, pattern, repetition, and color. Keeping all these elements in mind while making decisions might sound like a tall order, but in essence it means choosing elements that look the best together.

For example, in this Japanese garden, the shape of the container is reminiscent of a bonsai tray, but it's deeper, which makes it easier to maintain because it won't need daily watering. The 'Jervis' dwarf Canada hemlock has a graceful bonsai-style shape. Grass and ferns often appear in Japanese gardens, so the dwarf mondo grass and brass buttons, with their contrasting textures, were perfect candidates for this garden, with red thyme providing the lowest layer of greenery. The size of the garden is nicely balanced with stones, a pond, and a sand garden. Color and pattern are delivered with the red bridge, which might be a little predictable, but it's traditional and if you find one with the perfect fit, why not go with it?

Your next stop: Japan.

An arched wooden bridge with decorative balustrades is characteristic of traditional Japanese gardens.

This garden came together slowly. The garden bed was the first and easiest element to settle on, but the rocks, pond, bridge, and sand garden turned out to be a puzzle to fit together in one pot. Settling on a pond as a main feature helped the rest of the design fall into place. When you're sorting out different ideas for your miniature gardens, let the problems that you come up against work themselves out organically, instead of trying to force the pieces into place. Time is your creative ally.

ZEN SAND GARDEN

A traditional feature of Japanese gardens is a sand garden. You often see a sand garden in miniature in a tray, with no other elements, but adding it to an existing miniature garden makes both the sand garden and the living garden even more appealing. The sand used in this project is white sand, which you can find at a craft store in the floral section, or in the aquarium section of a pet store (keep in mind that white sand eventually gets dirty). Any fine sand will work here.

Find the rocks for this project at a local rock yard or garden center. They are usually sold by weight; hunt around for smaller pieces among the big pallets. Choose rocks that are the right size for the scale of your project. For example, this project is a half-inch scale, so rocks that are roughly 1 × 2 inches are a good fit. Pick up more rocks than you think you'll need and get a variety of shapes. This garden has about 18 rocks underneath the bridge and around the pond. Choose an interesting rock for the center of the sand garden. Use landscape cloth, not black plastic, underneath the sand. Landscape cloth will let rainwater drain and will hold the sand in place.

TOOLS AND MATERIALS

Planted miniature garden (with rocks and pond, if using, in place)

Landscape cloth, enough to cover the area in one solid piece

Scissors

Sand

Rocks, different sizes and shapes

Miniature rake

Layers and levels in the miniature garden.

INSTRUCTIONS

1 Line the area for the sand garden with the landscape cloth and trim off any excess cloth.

2 Tuck the edges of the cloth underneath the rocks, under the edge of the pond, and make sure it lines the outer edge of the pot.

3 Place the rock that will be the focal point on the landscape cloth. Leave enough room around the rock to be able to draw a miniature rake around it. Give consideration to which side of the rock is up: it is meant to look like a mountain.

4 Cover the area around the rock with the sand, a little at a time, until the landscape cloth is covered with a layer of sand ½ inch deep.

5 If any landscape cloth is sticking up, gently poke it into the soil. Try not to fuss with it too much at this stage; you don't want soil to spill into the sand garden.

6 Place the remaining rocks around the edge of the sand garden to hide the cloth.

7 Create a pattern in the sand by drawing a rake through the sand. Enjoy a moment of Zen.

PROJECT
EASY BONSAI PRUNING

Bonsai is an art. To master bonsai requires years of study, patience, and diligence, but thankfully, you can get a good taste of the art of bonsai from miniature gardening because the dwarf and miniature trees used are often the same plants that bonsai artists use, and they become even better specimens for bonsai as they grow older. After a couple of years, their trunks thicken, their branches get bigger and hold the leaf canopy up and out, and they begin to look like a full-size tree but in miniature.

It's easier than you might imagine to grow a tree that looks as though it has undergone years of training. Here we'll review a few pruning techniques that will help you train your trees to look like a bonsai tree. With these simple pruning techniques, you can dramatically transform a shrub into a tree.

You can trim your little tree like a bonsai. This one is a 'Jervis' dwarf Canada hemlock.

Miniature gardening is closer to penjing than to bonsai. The difference is in their names, as penjing means "pot of scenery" and bonsai means "planted pot." But it is the number of plants that separates these two ancient arts, and our miniature gardening is closer to penjing as miniature gardens are just that, a complete garden.

No special tools needed, just a sharp pair of small scissors.

INSTRUCTIONS

1 Always prune the branch, never cut the leaves.

2 Trim off any foliage or branches growing along or at the base of the vertical trunk. As you prune the trunk, decide which bigger branches to keep as you snip off the tiny branches.

3 Pinch or cut all foliage growing directly on the major trunks or branches.

4 Cut off any branch that is growing downward. Prune any branches that cross the center of the plant, or cross over another branch. Clip off any dead or dying branches, any yellow or dead leaves.

5 Pinch off any growth on the inside bends of the branch, or in the corners of any V shape.

MAKE IT SPECIAL

A LITTLE BIRTHDAY WISH

Birthdays. Each one of us has them, and we want to make them special, but it can be hard to find just the right gift for your friends and family. Why not honor that special day and make a happy birthday memory by giving the gift of an unforgettable miniature garden?

Birthdays are a fantastic opportunity to try out your miniature garden ideas on someone else. You can use a new technique or idea that you've been thinking about, and you can use any extra plants you have on hand from your other miniature garden projects. By decorating the pottery yourself and by making your own accessories, you'll have more room in your budget for new plants. Here's an example of what you can do that is easy on the budget as well as a uniquely personal do-it-yourself idea that also makes a remarkable gift.

A perfect birthday cake for the gardener who has everything.

Decorating the Cake

Now here is where you need to curb your creativity and think about who is getting this garden; you don't want to paint it her least favorite color or a shade that will clash with her surroundings. In this project, the pot was decorated to look like a birthday cake with lace painted orange to look like fondant. At the very least, it is a festive container and the lowest-calorie cake ever.

You can find all kinds and styles of lace ribbon in most fabric stores these days as some very lovely lace trim and embellishments are less expensive and a lot less delicate than your grandmother's lace. You will be treating it with an outdoor stiffener to weatherproof it.

BIRTHDAY IDEAS FOR THE MINIATURE GARDEN

Use the recipient's favorite colors, movie, joke, hobby, or sport for an overall theme.

Include one of their hobbies, interests, or specializations, and put it on a pedestal.

Represent their children, pet, or yourself in the scene.

SHRINK WHAT?

This project uses Shrinky Dink, a fun line of craft kits based on a plastic that shrinks when you bake it in your oven. There are kid-friendly kits for making jewelry, ornaments, magnets, and buttons, or get a pack of blank sheets and make anything that you like.

Look carefully at the Shrinky Dink kit you're considering to make sure it is suitable for your printer because the kits have different kinds of sheets for different purposes. Organize the words or images on your computer, print the sheet, cut out the shapes, and bake them. The sheet shrinks by one third of its original size, so work backward to get the size that you want. For example, if you want a sign to be 2 inches across after it's baked, the Shrinky Dink sign should be 3 inches across before it's baked.

Here are some pointers for formatting words for your signs on your computer:

1. To maximize the amount of space you have to work with, set the margins as small as the computer will allow.
2. Leave space above and below each row, or make it double-spaced.
3. Use a variety of fonts for the signs.
4. Turn on the rulers so you know what size the words are on your screen.
5. After you print the sheet, use a hole-punch or a specialty stamp for different shapes and ideas.
6. Do a test printing using a regular sheet of paper first, so you don't waste a sheet of the Shrinky Dink.

Awesomeness in every direction.

PROJECT
A GOOD SIGN

This is a great gift to give anyone as a reminder of the wonderful things that happen every day. You can substitute your own words, of course, and the idea is adaptable for special occasions in addition to birthdays. A thank-you present could include signs saying "thank you" in different languages. A present for a milestone birthday could have the names of the recipient's friends and family on the signs as a snapshot or reminder of that special celebration.

TOOLS AND MATERIALS

Shrinky Dinks for inkjet printers

Thick cardboard, one or two pieces,
   8 × 10 inches each

Scissors

Five-minute epoxy glue

Dowel, staked

Paint tray

Paintbrushes

Acrylic paint in assorted colors

UV-protectant spray

INSTRUCTIONS

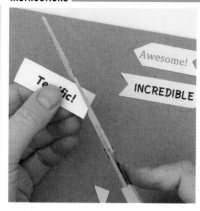

1 Print out your sign designs on a page of Shrinky Dink. Cut out the signs. Cut some arrows pointing to the left, some pointing to the right, and, on your favorite signs, cut arrows pointing in both directions.

3 If you like, you can paint the signs now, before you glue them to the dowel, although they are easier to handle once they've been attached to the dowel. Arrange the signs in the order you want them to appear on the dowel, then turn them over so that they're facedown on the work surface. Using the epoxy glue, and following the epoxy manufacturer's directions, glue the signs onto the dowel. Let dry, then paint each sign with a wash of color, then spray with a coat of UV-protectant spray.

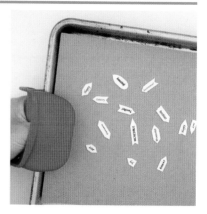

2 Preheat the oven to between 275°F and 300°F. Place a sheet of cardboard on a baking sheet, and place the signs on the cardboard. Place a sheet or two of cardboard on top of the signs and bake for 3 to 4 minutes. Remove the baking sheets from the oven and carefully press down on the top piece of cardboard with a spatula to flatten the signs, making sure that you press down over each sign. Return the baking sheet to the oven and bake for another 1 or 2 minutes. Remove the baking sheet from the oven, flatten down the signs again, and let cool.

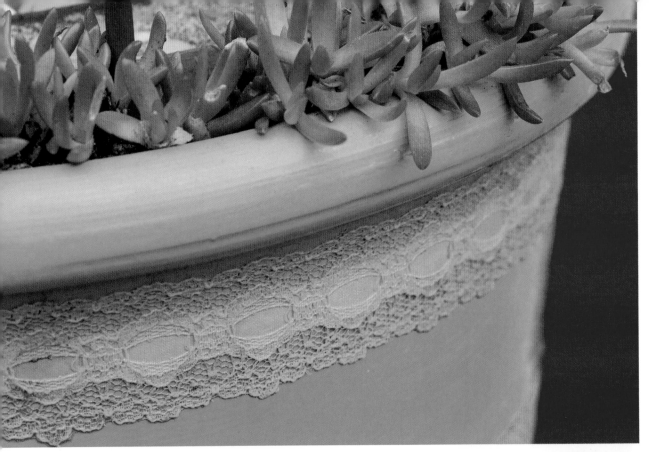

PROJECT
LET THEM PLANT CAKE

Terra-cotta pots are so popular, almost every garden has at least one some-where. Always start with a terra-cotta pot that is clean and dry. As long as it doesn't have a lot of mold on it, a dirty terra-cotta pot can be soaked in warm, soapy water with a splash of bleach to clean it. If you can't get the pot perfectly clean for this project, invest in a new one. Visit your local garden center for a variety of low-cost options and look for a pot with a shape that mimics the shape of a cake. To extend the life of the pot, it should be recoated a couple of times a year with Mod Podge for Outdoors, so be sure to visit the recipient and recoat the pot to give your gift a longer life.

↑ **Make the pot look like a layer cake with the plants as the frosting.**

TOOLS AND MATERIALS

Terra-cotta pot

Mod Podge for Outdoors

Paintbrushes, one large and one small

Acrylic paint in assorted colors

Paint tray

Lace ribbon, two or three kinds, enough to wrap around the pot

Clean, soft rag

1 Using the large paintbrush, seal the inside and outside of the terra-cotta pot with Mod Podge for Outdoors, following the manufacturer's directions. Then, using the large paintbrush, paint the pot with the color you've chosen for it. Depending on which brand of paint you're using, you may have to apply two coats of paint to get a solid coat of color. Let dry between coats.

2 For each ribbon you're using, measure how much ribbon you'll need to wrap around the pot and cut the ribbons accordingly. Using the small paintbrush, paint each length of ribbon a different color, using the same color for both sides of the ribbon. Let dry.

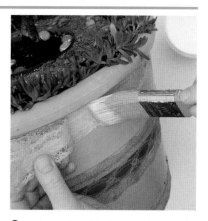

3 Apply Mod Podge for Outdoors to the areas on the pot where the ribbons will be placed. Wrap a ribbon around the pot on the wet Mod Podge and paint over it with more Mod Podge, making sure that the entire surface of the ribbon adheres to the pot. Repeat with the remaining ribbons. Let dry.

4 Paint the pot and ribbons once again with another coat of the Mod Podge for Outdoors. Let dry. Treat the pot a couple of times a year for maintenance.

Applying colorful paint, plus some ribbons, is a fun and easy way to jazz up a pot.

AN ENCHANTING GARDEN WEDDING

It's time to create your dream wedding. It will be a small wedding, miniature, in fact, but it will be all yours. Stage it exactly how you like, with the perfect flowers, in a perfect garden, and on a perfect day. Okay, that may be too much to ask, but you can certainly use this project to design the elements that would make a special wedding day. Planning a wedding can be stressful, but here you can plan *and* get a little garden therapy at the same time.

A garden wedding hosted in a backyard, botanical garden, or a favorite park is a popular option instead of holding the special occasion in an indoor venue, making a wedding even more fun to replicate in a miniature garden. First, focus on finding or building three main elements of the area. Then simplify further by creating a vignette of just the ceremony area rather than trying to squeeze a whole day's events in one container. Consider trees that you can miniaturize, suitable fences, and the shape of the garden beds first, then simplify the overall layout. Remember the adage that less is more and don't clutter the scene with too many details.

Enjoy getting the wedding details just right.

If you have a real wedding on the horizon, you can use this miniature garden as a centerpiece for one of the tables at the reception, but be sure to plant the garden a few months in advance of the big day so that it has time to grow in by then. If you plant the garden well ahead of time, it will be one less item on your busy to-do list. For most regions, an outdoor miniature garden needs less maintenance than one for indoors, and a wider selection of trees can be drawn from.

Symmetrical Gardens

Creating a symmetrical garden is a fun challenge. Once you find the right trees and shrubs to anchor the beds with, the bedding plants will fall into place easily. Symmetry can add drama to a focal point. In this garden, the bedding plants are white cranesbill (*Erodium ×variabile* 'Album'), the altar area is framed by two tall and bushy 'Sky Pencil' hollies which are framed by fairy vines (*Muehlenbeckia complexa*, also called maidenhair vine). Using tiny pops of color in the flower arrangement will help draw the viewer's eye to it.

Once the plants are chosen, the design stage can begin. Get a ruler out to make it easy to divide the pot in half to keep the design symmetrical. When you're trying to estimate so many variables in one layout without the correct measurements, a ruler helps prevent you from missing something. Another good idea is to plant

Plant the garden
well ahead of time
so the plants have
time to settle in
and look their
best.

A tiny mosaic bead stands-in for "something old."

your garden and then wait at least one day before finalizing the design. By taking a short break from the garden you will be able to see any oversights, such as not leaving enough room for chairs for the guests, or you will notice another way to bring the wedding colors into the scene, and you can make changes easily.

Something Old, Something New

Enjoy the challenge of miniaturizing wedding traditions. Wedding decor comes in all shapes and sizes in the full-size world, so why not go for it in miniature? Replicate the popular saying, "Something old, something new, something borrowed, and something blue" in your miniature garden and add charming details for viewers to enjoy. Most details can be handmade, or else look for them at a dollhouse store or online.

The pot used for this garden is a version of the Let Them Plant Cake project, except that this one is painted white. A word of caution if you are planting this garden well ahead of your wedding and want to use it as a centerpiece: keep the finished white pot off the ground. Put it on a pedestal or table until the special day, or the pot will get dirty really fast. The pot color is also a great opportunity to tie in your wedding colors, too.

Don't be afraid to invest in this scene either. Why not make it lovely enough to hold a place of honor at a wedding? A wedding-themed miniature garden can be used in a number of areas at the reception: the welcome table, bar, or lounge area, or put it on a table with the guest book. Full-size greenery and flowers can be nestled around the base of the pot to hide the electrical cord for the lights.

With the help of a ruler, symmetry is easy to accomplish in a miniature garden.

PROJECT
MAKING ARCHES

These arches are for a wedding ceremony–themed garden, but they can be put to use in any garden that needs an architectural element. To find the kinds of branches that can be bent, research vines or branches that are popular for baskets, which are woven with freshly cut material that can bend easily without snapping; then look for new, green branches from those varieties. (If you're planning on featuring this garden at a real wedding, source the branches a few weeks before the big day because the branches need three to four weeks to dry out.) Grapevine branches are ideal for making arches because they are thick enough to insert a stake into to support the arch in a garden bed. Honeysuckle, akebia vines, clematis, passionflower, or any ivy all have thinner branches, so if you're using any of those, twist several vines together to form an arch. Branches from a weeping birch or corkscrew willow also work well. Look around your full-size garden for different plants you can harvest, if you don't have vines, and look to the new growth on trees or shrubs.

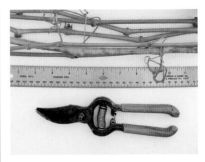

TOOLS AND MATERIALS

Sturdy cardboard box, about 8 × 10 inches

Branches or vines, about six to eight, 18 to 20 inches long

Ruler

Garden shears

INSTRUCTIONS

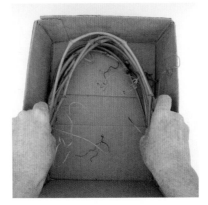

1 Bend the branches gently and gradually at the point that will be the apex of the arch. You will hear and feel fibers breaking as you do this. You'll be putting them into the cardboard box, so bend them only as much as you need to fit them into the box.

2 Gently put the bent branches in the cardboard box. Press them down if they start to pop up. Set the box aside until the branches dry. Let them dry for three to four weeks, although how long they'll need to dry out will depend upon how arid your environment is. You'll be able to tell by their change in color or by the way they stay in a U-shape that they're ready to use.

PROJECT
LET THERE BE LIGHT

What is more magical than a lighted archway? A lighted archway in miniature! Here, we'll take the grapevine arches and turn them into three arches for the ceremony spot.

TOOLS AND MATERIALS

Dried grapevine arches

Ruler

Drill with ¹⁄₁₆-inch bit

Metal rods, about 4 to 5 inches long

Epoxy glue

String of small battery-powered LED
    lights, 13 feet long on wire

Scissors

**Wedding arches
give you a perfect
excuse to include
miniature lights.**

INSTRUCTIONS

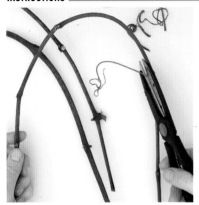

1 Using the garden shears, snip off any tendrils or rough stubs from the grapevine arches. The arches should be as smooth as possible.

2 Choose three arches that best match each other in size and shape. Line them up on a table and trim them all to the same length.

3 Using the drill, drill a hole into both ends of each arch 2 to 3 inches deep. Insert a metal rod into each hole. If the stakes don't fit tightly in the holes, dip the stake in epoxy glue before inserting it into the arch.

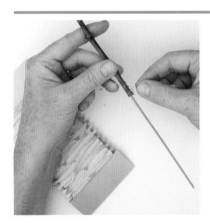

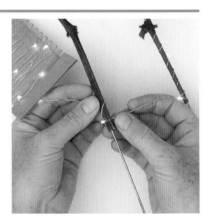

4 Starting at the base on one side of an arch, and leaving enough wire from the battery pack end of the light string to let it hang off the side of the pot, wind the light string around the arch.

5 Turn the lights on so you can see where the lights are landing on the arch as you wind the string around the arch. When you get to the end of the arch, wrap the string of lights a couple of times around the end of the arch to fasten it so it won't unwind.

6 When you finish wrapping the lights around the first arch, leave 1½ to 2 inches of lights unwound so that you have enough length to reach to the next arch. Make the length longer or shorter, depending on how far apart you'll be placing the arches.

7 Repeat steps 4 through 6 for the remaining two arches. Starting with the first arch that you attached the lights to (the one with the end of the light string that has the battery pack), install the arches in the garden by inserting the metal rods into the soil to secure the arches in place. The end with the battery pack should hang down the back of the pot. Hide the other end and any other visible sections of wire among the plants in the garden bed.

Wrap the arches in tulle to make them more romantic.

MAKE IT MAGICAL

Wrap the the arches in tulle ribbon to diffuse the lights and make the scene even more magical. Look for tulle ribbon in the wedding department of your local craft store. It's available in many colors, so you should be able to find the right colors for your wedding scene easily. Wrap the arches the same way that you wrapped the lights, starting at one end and working from one arch to the other. Or, wrap the arches individually and use a tiny piece of floral wire at each end to fasten the tulle in place. Don't place the wrapped arches in the garden too far ahead of the big day or the sun and rain may weather the tulle.

Design a huge arrangement for the special day to place at the center of your wedding scene.

PROJECT
WEDDING BOUQUET

The tiny flowers used for this floral arrangement were taken from large artificial sprays found in a craft store. Large craft stores usually feature aisles of artificial greenery, garlands, and floral sprays that are meant for full-size decorating purposes, and if you look closely at the greenery, you can see that they are made up of many parts that are mounted on plastic stems. Look for smaller flower and leaf parts that you can pull apart or cut off for the arrangement. Choose your wedding colors if you can, but if they're not available, choose white flowers and paint them.

Here, artificial baby's breath with tiny white flowers is just the right size for the main flower in the arrangement. The arrangement is trimmed with green, glitter-covered leaves. Silver and white floral stems, sequined and beaded filler sprays, and painted seedpods fill in the bouquet.

The base of the bouquet is floral Styrofoam, which you can find at any craft store. You can use any type of Styrofoam, but the stems of the plastic greenery are easy to poke into green or white floral Styrofoam. Oasis floral foam, which is often used for cut-flower bouquets, does not work very well for this project. If you have any trouble poking the plastic stems into the Styrofoam, try poking it first with a thin metal rod, then inserting the stems.

The stand that the flower arrangement sits on is a cake topper found in the wedding section of a craft store. It's spray painted blue to match the other wedding colors. You could also use vases that are about 2 inches wide by 3 inches tall, or big enough to hold a fabulous miniature bouquet.

In full-size flower arranging, the greenery is usually placed first, followed by the flowers and focal points. For this arrangement, you will build the bouquet from the back to the front so that you can get your fingers into the middle of it. Balance the colors of the flowers as you fill in the bouquet to make sure they are evenly dispersed.

TOOLS AND MATERIALS

Variety of artificial full-size floral sprays, filler, and greens

Dried seed pods, painted

Vase or miniature pedestal with a hole to hold the Styrofoam

Floral Styrofoam to fit your pedestal or vase

Floral wire, about 3 feet

Paint tray

Paintbrush, small

Acrylic paint in colors to match your wedding colors

Sharp knife

Scissors

Wire cutters

Clean, soft rag

MATERIALS USED FOR THIS FLORAL ARRANGEMENT

Twenty leaf stems

Fifteen green glitter stems

Eight white flower stems

Six blue flower stems

Two pink flower stems

Five long flowers: three white, two pink

Eight ball shapes: four rose colored (seed pods) and four blue (Styrofoam balls)

Painted spirals (grapevine tendrils)

Ribbons

Mini but magnificent: tiny sprigs mimic a grand floral arrangement.

INSTRUCTIONS

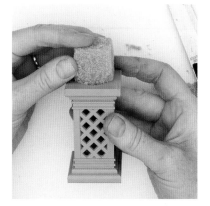

1 If you are painting your flowers, paint them first. Water down the paint so it is the consistency of yogurt, and load up the paintbrush with paint so that you can push paint into the middle of the flowers. To achieve a solid color on some types of plastic flowers, you may need to apply two or three coats of paint. Let dry between each coat.

2 Using a sharp knife, trim the Styrofoam to a size and shape that fits snugly in the hole of the pedestal or vase you're using, leaving at least 1¼ inch of Styrofoam above the edge of the pedestal or vase to work with. You can hot-glue this in after you are done, if needed.

INSTRUCTIONS

3 Using the wire cutters, cut a 6- to 8-inch piece of floral wire. Bend one end of the wire over itself, about 2 inches, and crimp the end to strengthen the wire.

4 Begin to wrap the crimped end of the wire around the stem of a flower spray to lengthen and strengthen the plastic stem so it is strong enough and long enough to poke in the Styrofoam.

5 Go through all your full-size sprays and snip off any flowers or foliage that you think you will need for your bouquet. Tie a longer wire onto each flower.

6 Determine which side of the pedestal will be the front. Some pedestals have the manufacturer's name on one side; make that side the back of the pedestal so that it's not visible from the front of the garden. Start to build the arrangement by inserting a row of long leaf stems into the back area of the Styrofoam first. It may be easier to glue the Styrofoam in place before you begin making the arrangement, but you might prefer to insert the stems into the Styrofoam before placing the bouquet into the pedestal.

7 Working row by row, insert the tall flowers in front of the row of greenery, then shorter flowers in front of the tall ones until you have a composition that you like.

8 When you reach the front of the arrangement, insert short stems of greenery into the front, left, and right sides of the Styrofoam, with their tops pointed down, so that they appear to hang down over the pedestal.

9 Finish the arrangement by adding accents such as painted balls, sprays of glitter stems, spirals, and ribbons tied in bows. If necessary, lengthen and strengthen the stems of the accent stems with wire, as described in steps 3 and 4. Balance these textures throughout the bouquet. Congratulations! You are a wedding designer in miniature!

Make small versions of the floral arrangement to decorate the benches. Lengthen the stems with wire so that you can attach the mini version to the bench, and cover the wire with floral tape. You can also make smaller bouquets to mark the start of the aisle, line the aisle, or place at the ends of each row of seating.

Garden benches are embellished with a flower, adding a touch of tiny perfection to the wedding scene.

MOTHER'S DAY

Instead of giving your mother just one bouquet on her special day, why not create an entire garden filled with tiny bouquets? A miniature garden by itself is a delightful gift, but when you add a few miniature flower arrangements, it just gets prettier. Create a tiny centerpiece for the table or an urn for a corner of the patio. Liven up a bare spot in the garden bed or use a mini bouquet as a distraction to take the focus off of a dormant plant. The tiny arrangements can be placed around the house or used as place-setting gifts at your next party.

Before you begin, take a moment to think about the type of bouquet you want to make. Will it be a cluster of the same flower nestled in some greenery? Or a rustic, country arrangement featuring woody stems, evergreen shoots, and trailing ivies? The real fun in making miniature flower arrangements is that it doesn't take long to make one, and you can experiment with different arranging styles in less than an hour.

Tiny Flowers Everywhere

Searching for tiny flowers, young leaves, and small branches to use in this project is a great way to appreciate Mother Nature's smallest details. Collect material from your garden, taking one to three stems from each

Have a little fun on Mother's Day.

plant, but resist picking everything at once. You won't need many stems to fill up the tiny vases, and you can always go back to the garden to collect more if needed. Bring a pot of water with you to put the blooms in if you are making a bigger bouquet; otherwise you can gather the flowers and greenery for one or two arrangements in one hand.

Flowering groundcovers, rockery plants, herb flowers, and miniature roses are great plants from which to harvest small flowers. Some full-size perennial flowers can be used as well; look for plants that send up tiny sprays of blossoms, like saxifrage and coral bells.

A Little Greenery

Searching for greenery can be as much fun as looking for flowers. Using foliage in your miniature arrangements will add texture and dimension and also highlight the blooms. Darker foliage adds depth, and light-colored foliage adds emphasis. Mix up larger foliage with smaller foliage so that the arrangement doesn't look messy.

Miniature and dwarf conifers from your miniature garden can be a great resource for miniature flower arrangements. Cut one or two branches from the back or bottom of the shrubs so their absence won't be noticed. Different kinds of conifers have completely opposite textures to small-leafed broadleaf plants like English boxwood and euonymus and contrast well with each other.

a. 'Helmond's Pillar' barberry

b. lady fern

c. Japanese andromeda

d. wall germander

e. 'Golden Devine' barberry

f. 'John Creech' sedum

g. 'Little Heath' Japanese andromeda

h. 'County Park Fire' podocarpus

i. boxleaf euonymus

j. ornamental grass

a. London pride (*Saxifraga umbrosa*)

b. variegated hardy geranium (*Geranium macrorrhizum*)

c. 'Bullata' Japanese spirea

d. 'Primuloides' miniature London pride (*Saxifraga* 'Primuloides')

e. 'Delight' parahebe

f. 'Charlie Brown' miniature rose

g. pink sea thrift (*Armeria alliacea*)

h. 'Amethyst Mist' coral bells

You will find many tempting color combinations in miniature.

The green leaves from parsley or rosemary are sturdy and will not wilt soon after picking. Miniature ivies or wire vines can cascade down a vase gracefully. The tops cut from any type of ornamental grass add wisps of whimsy.

If you don't have tiny flowering plants in your garden, collect small dried buds, skinny branches, or tiny, mossy twigs through winter and early spring and save them to use for Mother's Day. Substitute these for flowers to add details to your greenery. For a pop of vibrant color, paint them with an acrylic paint.

Sourcing Vases and Vessels

It is helpful to have a variety of small containers and vases on hand for whipping up a bouquet on Mother's Day (or any other occasion). Dollhouse stores, thrift shops, antiques shops, and some artist or craft markets are a few places to find a small vessels that can be used as a vase in a miniature garden. Search your kitchen for salt and pepper shakers, shot glasses, small liquor bottles, incense holders, and candleholders; these vessels can all be put to work as a vase. Toy kitchen accessories, miniature baskets, tiny baby carriages, and bathtubs meant for dollhouses can all be used as vases and lend a range of themes to a Mother's Day garden. Poke around your potting bench and garden shed for tiny pots, empty snail shells, and small bowls; they can all be put to use.

There is always room somewhere for a tiny vase of flowers.

White and glass containers provide a strong contrast with colorful flowers and greenery.

These tiny pots and vases, in various shades of blue and green, add a touch of realism to your miniature garden.

A dollhouse coffeepot makes an excellent miniature vase for a simple arrangement of three small green fronds and a colorful flower.

COUNTRY GARDEN POSY

As you work on this project, keep in mind the size of the vase you're working with and where it will be placed in your Mother's Day garden; you may need to gather more or fewer flowers and greenery than what is suggested here. As with full-size flower arranging, trim the bottommost leaves from the stems so they will not rot in the vase; trimming the leaves also helps extend the life of the bouquet. Remember to handle the tiny blooms delicately.

TOOLS AND MATERIALS

Wide-mouthed vase or small bowl

Scotch tape

Scissors

Small scissors

Three to five different textures of green filler (leaves, branches)

Three to five different textures of colored leaves

Three different blooms

Three different dried textures (seed pods, tiny branches, grapevine tendrils)

Tweezers

Turkey baster

INSTRUCTIONS

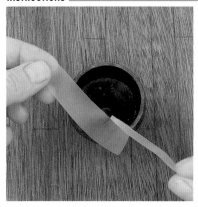

1 Cut or tear off a piece of Scotch tape long enough to fit across the mouth of the vase. Using scissors, cut the piece of Scotch tape into six or seven long narrow strips. Hang the strips by one end from the rim of the vase or the edge of the table as you cut them to keep track of them.

2 Stretch three or four of the strips across the mouth of the vase about ¼ inch apart. Turn the vase 90 degrees and make a grid of tape strips by stretching the remaining strips across the mouth of the vase about ¼ inch apart. Make sure the strips of tape are stuck securely to the vase's rim and stay in place. Using the small scissors, trim off any tape that hangs down too far (but be sure that the ends of the strips of tape are secured to the rim of the vase).

INSTRUCTIONS

3 Start building the arrangement using the larger green stems first. Using the small scissors, trim any leaves from the bottom of the stems, or pinch them off gently with your fingernails. To start the asymmetrical design, insert the stems into holes on one side of the grid.

4 Continuing to work on the one side of the vase, start introducing colored foliage or flowers to the mix, working carefully from the side of the grid to the center. Use the tweezers to delicately push the tiny stems down in the vase if necessary.

5 Working on the opposite side of the vase from where you started, begin layering in taller stems. If you have multiple stems of the same plant, keep them together within the same arrangement or balance them throughout the arrangement. Fill in the arrangement using the rest of your stems. Add the pops of color last, with flowers, painted branches, or colorful seed pods, and tuck in the trailing greens to cover up any visible tape. If needed, place some sturdy sprays of greenery at the back of the arrangement to help fill in bare spots and bring the foliage together to make it look fuller. Use the turkey baster to fill the vase with water at the back of the arrangement. The turkey baster will help direct the water through the flowers and tape without spilling any.

PROJECT
HANGING FLOWER VASE

A handmade hanging vase adds another layer of whimsy to a Mother's Day miniature garden. Hung empty, it provides a splash of color among the tree's foliage, or you could ratchet up the charm by placing a couple of tiny flowers or sedum cuttings in it. Making miniature vases with your mother is a memorable way to spend Mother's Day, and there is ample room for improvisation with color combinations.

For this project you'll use polymer clay to make a vase and cover it with a pattern and tiny roses and vines. Polymer clay is baked in the oven at a low temperature and hardens within half an hour, so the results are fast. You can always bake the vase again if you want to add more embellishments to it, but keep in mind that when it comes to design, less is more. For something as small as this vase, keep the design simple for the best results. The cloth mesh that creates the pattern on the vase can be substituted with lace or any type of screen, or you can impress a pattern on it with your hands.

Make different sizes of hanging vases for different places in the garden or your home.

WORKING WITH POLYMER CLAY

To get the best results when you're working with polymer clay, here are some guidelines.

- Work on a smooth work surface. If you don't have a smooth work surface, create one by taping waxed paper to a table.
- Warm up the clay by kneading it for a couple of minutes to make it supple.
- Be sure to check the baking directions on the packaging before going ahead with this method as some brands may have different directions.

INSTRUCTIONS

TOOLS AND MATERIALS

Polymer clay for the vase, ½-inch-square cube

Polymer clay for the flower, ¼-inch-square cube

Polymer clay for the vine, ¼-inch-square cube

Columnar shot glass or rolling pin

Ruler

Cloth mesh, 2½ × 1¼ inches

Metal nut pick or skewer

Glass or ceramic baking dish

Wire cutters

Round-nose pliers

26-gauge wire or lighter, about 10 inches long

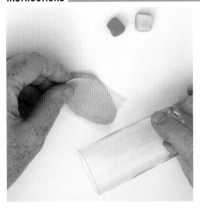

1 Using a columnar shot glass or rolling pin and working on a smooth surface, roll the clay for the vase into an oval shape about 2 inches long. Lay the mesh down on the rolled-out clay, then roll over the mesh to impress the pattern into the clay. Remove the mesh carefully.

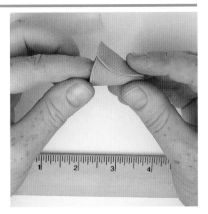

2 Create a cone shape by lifting one side of the oval and overlapping it with the other side.

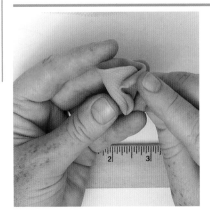

3 Using your finger, take the piece of clay that overlaps and turn the top edge down, creating a small curl. Curl the top rim of the vase downward. Measure the size of the vase; it should be less than 1 inch long for a large-scale miniature garden. If it is too big, roll the clay into a ball and start over with step 1.

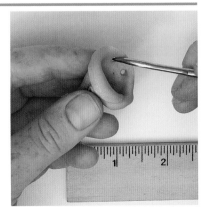

4 Using the nut pick or a skewer, poke two holes in the back of the vase, side by side, about ⅟₁₆ inch in diameter and about ¼ inch apart.

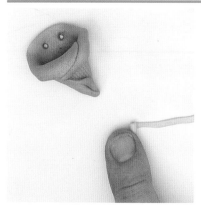

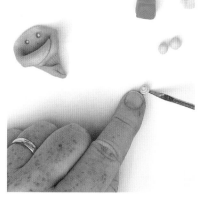

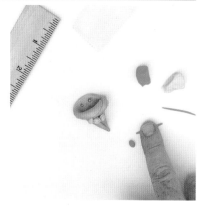

5 Divide the clay you're using for the flower detail into three pieces and roll them into balls about ³⁄₁₆ inch in diameter (if you have too much clay in a ball, then break some off). Use a fingertip to roll each ball into a log about ¹⁄₁₆ inch thick and about 1 to 1½ inches long. Flatten the clay along one side with the side of a fingertip. Starting at one end, roll the strip along the flat side from one side to the next with your finger to create the flower.

6 Use the nut pick or skewer to pick up the rose and place it on the front of the vase and close to the curled rim. Repeat steps 5 and 6 for the remaining two flowers, positioning the roses in a row underneath the rim of the vase. (Using an odd number of flowers makes a more interesting design.)

7 Divide the clay you're using for the vine detail into three pieces and roll them into balls about ³⁄₁₆ inch in diameter (if you have too much clay in a ball, then break some off). Use a fingertip to roll each ball into a log about ¹⁄₁₆ inch thick and 1½ inches long.

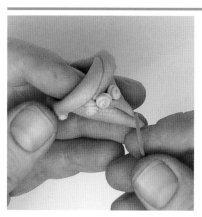

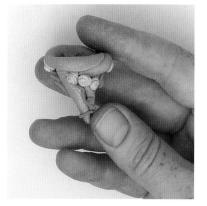

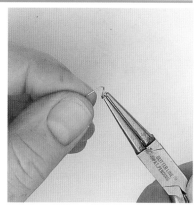

8 Starting at the bottom of the cone, carefully wind a vine loosely up the vase, turning the vine as you work upward to make it look like a tendril. The clay vine will stick to the vase as you place it. Repeat with the other two vines.

9 Place the vase in the baking dish and bake according to the directions on the polymer clay package. You can't overbake the clay, but it will turn brown if you leave it in the oven for too long. Some clay brands may darken in color after baking.

10 Using the round-nose pliers, take one end of the wire and wind it around the pliers to make it look like a grapevine tendril.

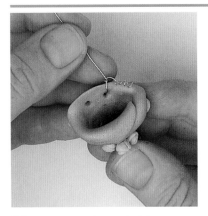

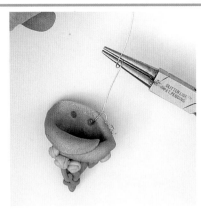

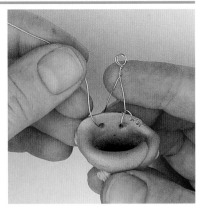

11 Thread the other end of the wire through one of the holes in the back of the vase. Pull it through to the point where the curly end hangs off to the side, then wrap it around itself.

12 Make a loop in the wire about ¾ inch up from the hole by wrapping the wire around the pliers, then twist the wire onto itself. This is what you will hang the vase with.

13 Pull the other end of the wire through the second hole in the vase, looping it around itself to fasten it to the vase securely.

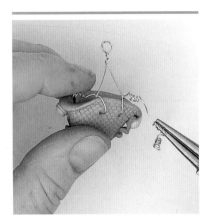

14 Curl the end wire into a tendril and position the tendril to hang down the other side of the vase. Now go pick some flowers from your garden and see how they will look in your miniature vase.

Pretty little details make Mother's Day special.

INDEPENDENTLY YOURS

There are a number of ways to represent summer in a miniature garden, but a special Fourth of July–themed miniature garden evokes a summertime gathering filled with food, family, and fireworks. When Independence Day comes around, you know that summer is here and it's time to kick back and enjoy the warm weather, barbecues, and summertime fun. When you plan your garden design, leave enough space for entertaining and cooking outdoors. The garden will create the backdrop for your scene, so don't scrimp on the trees and plants; rather, fit the accessories into your design in different ways, like starting with a larger plot or container and making a bigger patio area for a table of four and a barbeque. Make use of an empty spot in between plants for a wading pool or tiny sandbox, or decorate the trees with summer-themed garlands or ornaments hung on branches. If you're short on space, consider taking your cue from the birthday project and decorate the pot.

Backyard Design Ideas

A miniature backyard garden design can be as simple as a big 'Jacqueline Hillier' Dutch elm planted with a lush lawn of Irish moss, or it can include perennial garden beds, paths going to and fro, and big shade trees in the corners. Create a courtyard with a wall of tall trees at the back of the garden and layer shorter plants in front with smaller plants around the sides and front to frame the scene nicely. Design a formal courtyard with a permanent patio made from square tiles locked in with Mini Patio Mix; or sink small pieces of flagstone right into the soil, flat side up, for a casual or rustic-looking patio. Either way, make the entertainment area big enough to eat, dance, and be merry.

The table is set, the lights are on, and the celebration is ready to start.

RE-CREATING MEMORIES FOR AN INDEPENDENCE DAY GARDEN

Independence Day, like any special occasion, can bring back fond memories for you and your family. Good times that were spent in your grandmother's backyard, playing horseshoes or croquet, can be replicated in miniature for everyone in the family to recall. You may be tempted to reproduce the scene exactly as you remember it, or perhaps use a favorite photo to inspire the design, but consider simplifying when you translate it to a living miniature garden.

When you are drawing on a memory or photo, choose one to three major components to reproduce in miniature to begin the project, then include more details as you come up with solutions for them. If you try to compose a picture-perfect scene all at once, it may be a bit daunting; remember, this is supposed to be fun.

Begin by choosing the main elements of the scene you want to make: was it the big tree in the backyard that was a central focus of your gatherings? Did everyone play a certain game each year? Or, perhaps it was Grandma, telling stories from her chair at the end of the table that the family remembers best? If you're creating this garden for a family gathering, you can make the get-together even more fun by making a miniature party favor for everyone to bring home.

The chair's patriotic hues really pop against the colors of the garden.

PROJECT
A PATRIOTIC PERCH

A backyard bash isn't complete without a comfortable chair or two. Adirondack chairs are quintessentially American, making them perfect for this project. This idea can be used for many other themes as the motif, stars, and colors can easily be interchanged for other motifs for other celebrations, as long as the icons on the armrests are recognizable in silhouette form. Look for stickers that are used for scrapbooking to find suitable candidates; you can find them at your local craft store or online. As you're planning the color scheme, keep in mind that the silhouette color is the primer, or first coat, for this project and the one that shows through when you're finished.

TOOLS AND MATERIALS

Wood Adirondack chair

Wood hardener

Disposable metal or glass container

Disposable paintbrush

Paintbrushes, one medium, one small

Acrylic paint in cherry red, white, and navy blue

Paint tray

Star stickers

Craft knife

Water

Clean, soft rag

INSTRUCTIONS

1 Wipe any dust or dirt off the chair. Pour a little wood hardener in the disposable container. Using the disposable paintbrush, paint the entire chair with the wood hardener, covering the top and bottom, and painting in between the slats. Let dry. Using the medium paintbrush, apply a coat of white paint, covering the entire chair once again. Because the star stickers will be placed on the armrests of the chair and the front of the seat, make sure these areas have a solid coat of paint on them. Let dry.

2 Place the star stickers on the armrests and backrest of the chair. Use a craft knife to help you position them in a straight line.

INSTRUCTIONS

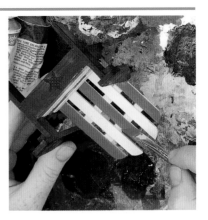

3 Use your fingers to press down firmly on the stickers to make sure all the parts of the stickers are adhered to the wood.

4 Using the smaller paintbrush, apply a coat of blue paint over the stickers, and paint any other parts of the chair that you would like to be blue. Let dry.

5 Using the small paintbrush, paint every other slat red, so that you have an alternating pattern of red and white on the seat and backrest. Let dry. Apply another coat of blue and red again if necessary to get a solid coat. Let dry.

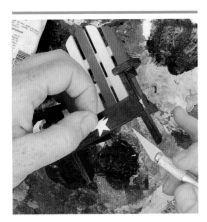

6 Slide the tip of the knife underneath a sticker and gently lift it off, being careful not to pull the paint off. Repeat with the remaining stickers. Touch up any white paint with the small paint-brush. Let dry. Send the invitations and plan the menu.

LIGHT UP YOUR LIFE

Lights allow your celebration to extend into the evening. Round out the garden scene by hanging a string of lights from post to post to give the patio a sparkly, festive appearance. In this project, you will make two different kinds of light posts: one that is a solid post that can endure a little tugging without dislodging, and another that is just meant to hold the string of lights in place. Miniature lights are available at miniature garden stores or craft stores. The small wood dowels and wire can be found at most hardware stores or at hobby and craft stores.

TOOLS AND MATERIALS

One package of miniature lights, 13 feet long

Eight dowels, ¼ inch × 8 inches long

20-gauge wire, 6 inches long

Four metal rods, ¹⁄₁₆ inch × 3½ inches long

Four small disposable cups

Drill with ¹⁄₁₆-inch bit

Flat-nose pliers

Round-nose pliers

Wire snips

Silicone glue

Mini Patio Mix, 2 pounds

Sturdy miniature posts with hooks make stringing the lights easier and add atmosphere to the scene.

INSTRUCTIONS

1 Make a hook. Using the round-nose pliers, bend one end of the 20-gauge wire into a small U-shaped hook. Using the flat-nose pliers, bend the loop backward, making a 90-degree bend. Close the U-shape a little with the round-nose pliers, leaving a ¹⁄₁₆-inch gap for the light string.

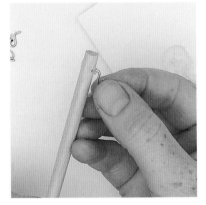

2 Snip the completed hook off the main wire, leaving a ⅜-inch stem at the 90-degree bend. Repeat seven more times to make eight hooks.

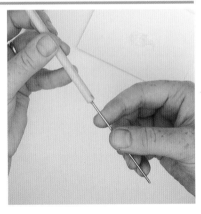

3 Using the drill, drill a hole in all of the dowels, about ⅜ inch from one end. It may be easier to drill the hole all the way through the dowel; either way will work. The end with the hole drilled in it will be the top of the post.

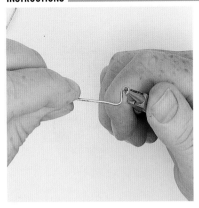

4 On four of the dowels, drill a hole into the end that will be the bottom. This hole is to stake the dowel with the metal rod.

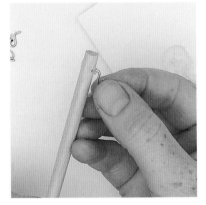

5 Squeeze a dab of glue onto a piece of scrap paper. Dab the straight end of the hook into the glue and insert the hook into the hole that was drilled near the top of each dowel, making sure the glue gets into the hole, too. Repeat with the remaining seven hooks. Make sure the opening of the hook faces up, so that it will hold the string of lights.

6 Dip one end of a metal rod into the glue and insert it into the hole that was drilled into the bottom of the dowel. Repeat with the remaining three rods and dowels.

7 Assemble the four cups and pour dry Mini Patio Mix in each cup, leaving about ½ inch of space at the top. Place one dowel, hook end up, into each cup. Tap the cup to get out any air pockets.

8 Gently fill the cups with water until the water starts to pool on the surface. The mix will start to bubble as air bubbles escape. Insert an unstaked dowel into each cup.

9 Carefully roll each cup between your hands to work the water down to the bottom of the cup to wet and activate the cement. Make sure the posts are centered and straight. Watch them for a few minutes until you're sure they won't move off center or tilt sideways. Let the mix dry for a few days, as cement-based Mini Patio Mix needs to cure slowly. Peel the cups off the hardened Mini Patio Mix once it has completely cured.

10 The dowels should alternate one staked dowel, then one cemented dowel. Determine the arrangement of the dowels around the patio and dig holes in the spots where you want to bury the four cemented dowels, then bury them firmly in the soil. Position the four staked dowels in between them. String the lights in the hooks and tuck the battery pack behind a bush, or tape it to the back of the pot. Turn them on. Get the cocktails.

Nestle the light post in the garden with a couple of strategically placed rocks to make it look natural.

A HAUNTED HALLOWEEN

Glowing jack-o'-lanterns, creaking porches, cobweb-draped windows and doors, and kids laughing and scaring each other willy-nilly are among the sights and sounds that make our spines tingle every October. Halloween is fun for everyone. But when it comes to the garden, full-size or miniature, there is only one very scary thing to make: a haunted graveyard.

Halloween in a miniature garden has a spirit all its own. Tiny, cobweb-covered gravestones and skeletons creeping around little pumpkin patches beckon everyone to come in for a closer look at the scene. You'll definitely see laughs and smiles from everyone, and maybe a few shivers. Be sure to put the garden beside the front door at eye level to keep the trick-or-treaters amused while they wait for their candy, if only for a moment. You will need an indoor one for your party, too.

Decorating with Decay

A Halloween garden is where your collection of faded and broken miniature garden accessories will come in handy. Just about anything that looks like it has seen better days can show up in a miniature graveyard, such as an old boot or a headless garden statue. Both could easily be found discarded in a corner of a cemetery. Any abandoned object that we regularly use, like clothing, a bottle, a toy, or a garden tool will start the story and have the viewer thinking, "Weird, what is that doing here?"

Scare up Halloween decorations in your usual haunts, but be sure to cruise the seasonal aisles wherever you shop; you might be surprised at what you will find. Six-inch-tall skeletons strung as a garland and skull-bead bracelets meant for costumes can be taken apart and used in a miniature garden. When you are in your favorite fabric or craft store, head to the button section and you'll find a wealth of ideas that can be mounted on lollipop sticks and transformed into spooky yard art. For realistic, in-scale miniature pumpkins, gravestones, black cats, and other resin decorations, visit your favorite miniature garden or dollhouse store.

Accessories not necessarily meant for Halloween can be adapted to fit perfectly into Halloween scenes, too. In this example, the white metal picket fence surrounding the cemetery was repurposed from a previous garden, beat up, painted, and made to look rusty to give it the appearance of having been there for decades. A tiny piece of fabric found on one of the fence pickets offers more intrigue, as if someone left the scene in a hurry. When you're placing the tombstones, put them in a bit crooked. If you want color in the scene, add pumpkins and squashes but pile them haphazardly. It's a haunted scene, so who knows what goes on there at night?

Everyone loves Halloween in miniature!

Save broken accessories to use in a haunted garden. The base holding this pumpkin head came from a broken birdbath.

Make the graves stand out by covering them with a moss that's different from the moss used for the lawn.

Make the scene a little unkempt. Zombies are untidy.

For more easy-to-find fodder for the scene, gather stones for miniature boulders to place in the back of the garden bed; they'll instantly add age and permanence to the vignette. Use a mossy branch as an old decaying tree trunk, or a few pieces of driftwood nestled in the soil. Add bits of moss to corners or wherever you need to fill in a bare spot around a gravestone. Make it less than perfect; after all, ghosts and zombies are terrible landscapers.

Planting Halloween

This project is an excellent example of how a dormant garden can temporarily be used to make a garden with another theme. Once the occasion is over, like Halloween, just remove the accessories. The garden in this project is an older miniature garden with dormant bedding plants. The understory was bare, leaving an area for a cemetery. The rich, gray color of the junipers is the perfect shade for the occasion, and the tall 'Compressa' juniper holds the ghosts high, making it seem like they are flying.

The cemetery looks like it is part of a bigger graveyard thanks to the Irish moss, which is carefully divided up in the right pattern to look like lawn, with enough space left for gravesites. A different type of moss tops the mounded graves to distinguish them from the lawn, and a row of stones around each grave helps define them.

Another frightening plant that you can use for your Halloween scene is corokia, a small shrub with a predominant zigzag branching habit and tiny leaves that looks like it came straight out of a fairy tale's haunted forest. Other plants that can be used for creepiness are carnivorous plants. Venus flytraps are the most well-known, but sundews, pitcher plants, and bladderworts have wonderful structure, texture, and colors.

PROJECT
A SPOOKY GHOST

Ghosts are classic Halloween spirits, and no self-respecting cemetery would be without at least one ghost. This ghost is made from tulle that was treated to hold its shape and to make it suitable for outdoor use. Tulle is a fine netting often used for wedding decor, and it gives this ghost an ethereal look. You can find tulle in almost any craft store that has a wedding section, and it's available in different ways, usually on a roll or in pre-cut circles (used for bouquets). If you can't find tulle, any type of light fabric will work for this project; feel free to use patterns and colors that match your theme to have a bit of campy Halloween fun. This ghost can be made to any scale you want.

You can make your ghost stand up by putting it on a rod, or attach it to dark green floral wire looped around the trunk of the tree so that it looks like it's flying. Create a host of ghosts to go in your full-size garden for more laughs.

A ghost made out of tulle seems to hover over the cemetery, while a piece of fabric caught on the fence adds more mystery to the scene.

TOOLS AND MATERIALS

White tulle

Ruler

Scissors

Wire cutters

28-gauge floral wire

Plate or bowl

Paintbrush

Mod Podge for Outdoors

Water

INSTRUCTIONS

1 Cut two pieces of tulle roughly 6 × 6 inches square. Cut it haphazardly around the edges to make them a bit uneven. Cut a 12-inch piece of wire and put it aside.

2 Gather the center of one of the pieces of tulle into a ball and place in the center of the other piece of tulle. Gather the outer piece of tulle around the inner piece to create the head of the ghost.

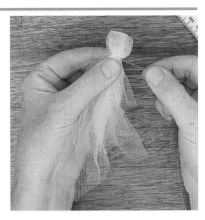

3 Pinch the neck of the ghost together tightly while you circle the wire once around the neck and twist the wire around itself to fasten it. Leave the ends of the wire alone.

4 Dip the ghost in water. Using the paintbrush, put a couple of dollops of Mod Podge on the tulle and work it through the fabric with your fingers.

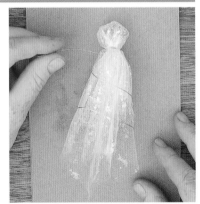

5 Wrap the wires loosely around the ghost's body to keep the tulle from splaying out too much while it dries. Let the tulle dry completely. Leave the wire uncut if you are hanging your ghost in a tree, or cut the ends of the wire close to the neck and twist them together tightly so that they don't poke out. Now the ghost is ready to haunt the garden.

PROJECT
REDUCE, REUSE, REVIVE FROM THE DEAD

Zombies can be created to show varying degrees of decay. For miniature figures that are dressed, customize them by painting on dirt, gluing moss into crevices, and finishing with some bloody fingertips and scratches. To mummify a zombie, wrap the figure in bandages, but leave some skin visible.

In this project, you will learn how to pin two tiny parts together to make a lasting join. This method requires drilling a hole in both pieces and joining them with a small metal rod and glue to create a strong bond that won't break easily. A statue of a bather whose head had broken off was a good candidate for this project. If you try to glue the tiny pieces back together without pinning them first, keeping them together while the glue dries will be tricky and the join will be very fragile. Pinning the head into the neck makes it easier to glue the pieces together and helps create a more secure bond. This technique works for attaching any small parts together. Also, staking the accessory beforehand will help you hold on to the figure more easily while you work.

↑ **Zombies come alive at night. Adding a young zombie can completely change the story.**

TOOLS AND MATERIALS

Broken miniature figure, staked

Small drill with ⅛-inch bit

Leather gloves (optional)

Small metal rod, 1/16 inch thick

Silicone glue

Sand, 1 tablespoon

Acrylic paint in white, lime green,
   Payne's gray, cherry red

Paintbrushes, small

Paint tray

Water

Fine-tipped black permanent marker

UV-protectant spray

Moss

Clean, soft rag

INSTRUCTIONS

1 Drill a hole in the neck of the figure's body, and another hole in the bottom of the head, as deep as you can, or at least ⅜ inch deep. If you are not confident drilling into such small pieces, wear a leather glove on the hand that you're holding the piece with; the leather will help you grip the tiny piece and it will protect your hand if the drill slips.

2 Cut a piece of metal rod to fit between the two pieces and fit it into the holes to see if it's the right length. If it's not, trim it and test it again until you have a length that fits the head and body together the way you want it to. Dip the rod into the glue, then insert it into the hole that you drilled in the body of the figure. Add a little glue to the end of the rod and insert it into the hole that you drilled in the head. Let dry.

3 Sprinkle sand on the wet glue to hide the excess glue and make the wound look decayed. If you have any big gaps to fill, glue a tiny piece of the moss to help fill the gap. Let dry.

4 Mix a small amount of white paint with a little water until the paint is the consistency of yogurt. Paint the entire figure and let it dry to tacky for a couple of minutes. Using the rag, gently dab off some of the excess white paint, especially on the figure's skin areas to make it look pale.

5 Paint the figure's hair and base Payne's gray. Darken the eye sockets, too. Paint the fabric green. Let dry.

6 Using a fine-tipped marker, draw veins on the statue's skin and face haphazardly. Paint the figure white again and dab off the excess paint with a rag to fade and age some of the veins.

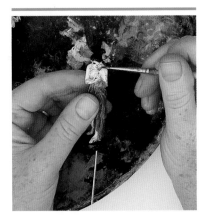

7 With a dry paintbrush and a little red paint, create scrapes and gashes over the zombie's skin. Use a smaller brush for more detailing. Let dry, then spray with UV-protectant spray. Prepare for your zombie apocalypse.

MUMMIFY YOUR ZOMBIE

1. Cut a few strips of white duct tape, about ⅛ inch wide and 2 to 3 inches long.

2. Wrap the duct tape around the figure's limbs to give the impression of decaying cloth.

3. Paint a wash of Payne's gray on the duct tape.

4. Dab off excess paint if needed, and let dry.

HAVE A MERRY LITTLE CHRISTMAS

The sights, sounds, and smells of the holidays are a feast for the senses. Christmas trees draped in colorful decorations and twinkly lights appear in shop windows and houses, excitement is in the air, and something magical may happen at any moment. It's Christmastime!

The holidays can be a perfect time for sharing your miniature garden hobby with friends and family. You can show off your miniature gardening skills by creating a special holiday-themed garden to put next to your front door, use as a centerpiece, or give as a gift.

In addition to decorating the tree in your miniature garden, you'll need some other embellishments to help balance the scene, just like you would for your full-size holiday decorating. Add a piece of holiday decor to the garden bed and you'll have a balanced display. The second project here is an easy-to-make miniature snowman, a perfect holiday character for a miniature garden.

Make Christmastime Ahead of Time

During the holidays it's hard to find time to do time-intensive projects. Fussing over tiny decorations while your to-do list is growing can be nerve-wracking. Sometimes it is hard to conjure the peace of mind for mini-making when there is so much else going on in your full-size world. How will you find time to tie little bows on a little tree? And how are you going to tie really small ornaments around tiny branches? Skip the tiny ornaments and decorations that you find in the craft stores (they're meant for those artificial tabletop trees anyway) and dress up a tree in this Christmas tree dress. You can make it well ahead of time, so you don't drive yourself nutty fiddling and fussing about with itty-bitty details when bigger things need your attention.

Decorate the garden, not just the tree.

Think of other characters to make in addition to a snowman.

Planting Christmas

In this outdoor full-sun miniature garden, a twelve-year-old 'Jean's Dilly' dwarf spruce keeps perfect company with the 'Mother Lode' juniper. The bedding plants in front of the spruce are hens and chicks, and a hardy groundcover, appropriately called ice plant, is on the left.

'Jean's Dilly', a variety of white spruce, is a smaller, denser, and slower-growing version of dwarf Alberta spruce. The growth rate averages about 2 inches per year, and some gardeners prune it to slow the growth even more, but remember that for every branch you cut at least two more will emerge so it may not keep its nice cone shape.

'Mother Lode' juniper is a hardy shrub that is a delight to grow and will keep you charmed throughout the year. It is a groundcover juniper, so it will only grow outward (or prostrate, not up), and it will maintain its height of 3 to 4 inches tall. Cut off any wayward branches just above a set of leaves to help disguise the cut. In the summer months, 'Mother Lode' juniper is a rich gray-green color that will turn amber and purple in winter where the temperatures dip to freezing.

Add some of your own twinkle, too.

BRING THE OUTDOORS IN

If you want to bring your outdoor miniature garden inside for a holiday display, treat it the same way as you would a full-size living Christmas tree and stage it before bringing it inside. Move the miniature garden to the garage or a covered porch for two or three days so that it can acclimate to a warmer temperature, then bring it into your home. If you can, leave it in a cool spot in the house for another day so that it can gradually adjust to the warm indoor temperature. If you bring it directly from the cold into your heated house, the tree may be so stressed by the difference in temperature that it may not recover.

Once the garden is inside, keep it away from any direct heat sources and out of the kitchen. Keep a close eye on it for any bugs that may wake up thinking it is spring. Do not mist it but keep the soil evenly damp. Remember to use a saucer to capture water that drains through and be careful of any saucer wicking on your wood furniture.

Tiny branches poke out from among the decorations.

PROJECT
A CHRISTMAS TREE DRESS

Once you've made this dress you'll be able to decorate your miniature Christmas tree in three minutes or less, making it look twinkly and colorful, almost like a present with a big bow on top. This is a perfect Christmas-in-July project, when you have the time to sit in your garden and make miniatures. For even more twinkle and sparkle, string a set of miniature lights on the tree first.

The tree dress is made with narrow ribbons, beads, tinsel garland, sewing notions, and a few miniature ornaments that can be easily found at craft stores, thrift shops, and sometimes even at garage sales. Be on the lookout for these trimmings throughout the year because the big-box stores do not carry narrow ribbons or tinsel garlands every year. Eight different kinds of ribbons and garland decorate the tree in this project, plus a couple of strands of ornaments.

The green wire that holds the dress at the base and at the top is plastic-coated heavy-duty garden wire that can be found at most hardware, craft, or garden stores. The wire is pinned in place while you work on it so get a cork board, a piece of sturdy cardboard, or a sheet of foam core that the wire can be securely pinned to.

A make-ahead idea that takes only minutes to install.

TOOLS AND MATERIALS

Cloth tape measure

Linesman's pliers

28-gauge green garden wire

Scissors

Ribbon, 8 to 10 different kinds, and bead or tinsel

Garlands, bead or tinsel

Straight ruler

Pushpins

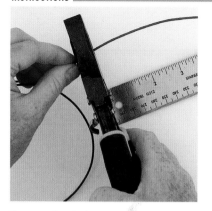

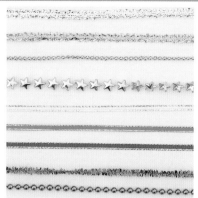

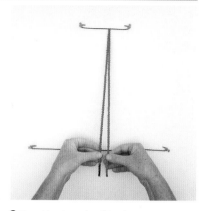

1 Using the cloth tape measure, measure the circumference of the tree loosely around the base of the foliage and just below the top of the tree (to leave some room for a bow or star). If you do not have a cloth tape measure, wrap a piece of string or ribbon around the tree in both places, then measure the length of the string with a straight ruler. In this example, the diameter at the top is 5 inches and the diameter at the bottom is 14 inches. Add about an inch to each measurement and cut the wire to those two lengths. Measure the height of the tree, too, and make a note of the measurement.

2 Measure and cut the ribbons and garland at least 2 inches longer than the height of the tree. In this example the tree is 28 inches tall, so the ribbons and garland are 30 inches long. You will use the extra 2 inches to tie them onto the other wire.

3 Bend both ends of both wires to make a hook shape. Pin the smaller wire near the top of the corkboard by pressing a pushpin through each hook. Pin the larger wire to the corkboard below the smaller wire, at a distance equal to the height of the tree (in this case, the distance is 28 inches). Loop a ribbon over the top wire and straighten it out so that the ends are even.

MINIATURE ORNAMENT STRINGS

Mixing in strings of miniature ornaments with the ribbons and garlands will add sparkle and texture to the tree dress. For rigid ornaments, like plastic candy canes, tie them onto thread. For anything that you can pierce with a needle, thread the needle and push it through the top of the ornament or wherever it makes sense in order for the ornament to hang well on the thread. Alternate the ornaments on the thread for additional interest.

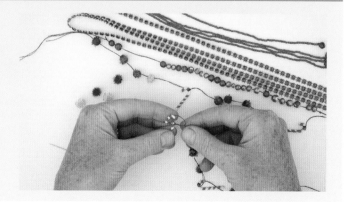

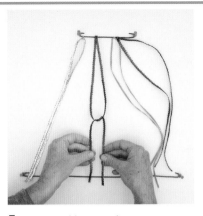

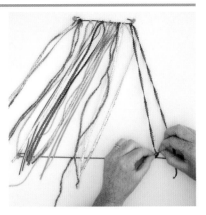

4 Holding the ribbon taut, with the ends even, make a loop to tie it in an overhand knot, and keep holding the ends as you tighten the knot around the wire.

5 Tie more ribbons to the top wire in any order you like. Make a repeating pattern or a random pattern; it's fine to move the ribbons around at this stage until you have a pattern you like. Don't worry about spacing them apart until you have finished tying all the ribbons to the top wire.

6 Begin tying the ribbons to the longer wire below, working from one end of the wire to the other. Twist each length of ribbon so that it makes a spiral and tie each end to the bottom wire. Once each ribbon is in place, tie a second knot to secure it.

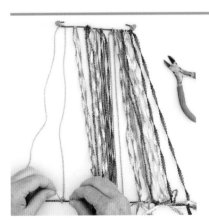

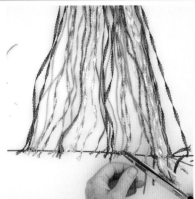

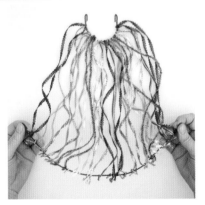

7 Tinsel garlands may need a more delicate knot; tie down any miniature bead garland strands with a small piece of wire.

8 Tie on more strands if you like. Trim the excess ribbon and trim off the bottom ends.

9 Unpin the two wires from the board. Bend each wire to make a circle and hook the hooks on each end together when you're placing the dress on the tree. Use your fingers to space the ribbons evenly around the tree. Get the eggnog!

PROJECT
A HOLIDAY SNOWMAN

This is an easy project in which a cardboard outline of a snowman is waterproofed, painted, and decorated. If you don't want to make a snowman, you can cut the cardboard into any fun shape, of course. Determine what size of a snowman will fit into your miniature garden before you begin. The stones for the eyes and mouth are micro pebbles. The carrot is from the dollhouse world. You can make these little accents from polymer clay if you like.

Yard art for the holidays!

TOOLS AND MATERIALS

Small piece of sturdy cardboard

Pencil

Scissors

Paint tray

Paintbrush

Paverpol

Popsicle stick

White acrylic paint

Superfine iridescent glitter

Red ribbon, 10 inches long

Craft knife

Tiny stones for the mouth and eyes

Miniature carrot

Clean, soft rag

INSTRUCTIONS

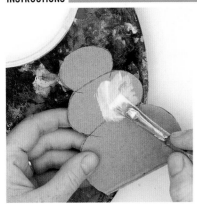

1 Draw the outline of a snowman on the cardboard and use the scissors to cut it out. Using a paintbrush, coat the front, back, and sides of the cardboard cutout with Paverpol. Be sure to brush Paverpol around the cut edges of the cardboard to make sure it is completely sealed. Let dry.

2 Use a dollop of Paverpol to glue the popsicle stick near the bottom of the side that will be the back of the snowman. The popsicle stick will be used to stake the snowman into the soil.

3 Apply a solid coat of white acrylic paint on the snowman. While the paint is still wet, sprinkle the surface with the superfine iridescent glitter and cover the front and edges. Tap off any excess glitter. Let dry.

4 Tie the red ribbon around the snowman's neck and use a dab of Paverpol to glue the knot in place. Arrange the scarf so that it hangs down from the neck and cut the ends of the ribbon at a length you like.

5 Carefully apply a coat of Paverpol to the ribbon, and apply another coat of Paverpol to the front, back, and cut edges of the snowman too. Let dry.

6 Using the knife, put a tiny dab of Paverpol on the snowman's face where you'll place the stones for the mouth and the eyes.

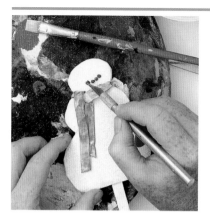

7 Clean off the knife and use it to move the stones to the right spots.

8 Cut off the wide end of the carrot, dip it into Paverpol, and place it on the snowman's face. Let dry.

9 You can add more embellishments at this stage, like a top hat, buttons, and twig arms. Once you are done, paint the front and back of the snowman, and the popsicle stick, with a thorough layer of Paverpol. Let it dry completely before placing it in your Christmas garden. Queue the Christmas carols!

MINIATURE IMAGININGS

FAIRY HAVEN

Has your fairy house seen better days? Is the paint faded and the fairies long gone? Are you thinking about getting a new house, but don't want to discard the old one? It's too faded for the thrift store, and it's not broken so it's not garbage. If only there was a way to save it. Instead of buying a new fairy house, which would likely be made of resin and painted without regard to the bleaching effects of the sun, roll up your sleeves and give your old fairy house some new curb appeal. With some imagination and elbow grease, paint, glue, and fairy bling, you can rescue your fairy houses from the landfill, save a few dollars, have a great time creating something unique, and restore the magic to your old fairy house.

Most of the fairy houses on the market have a generic exterior, providing you with ample opportunity to improve upon the house's existing features. Start with the architectural details, and enhance them with a color palette of your choosing. For example, if there are shutters on the windows, use them as an opportunity to have some fun with a blast of color. Door frames can be detailed, window boxes painted bright colors, and brickwork can be highlighted with different shades.

Thatched roofs can be painted brown with yellow highlights to refresh their straw-like appearance, or they can be highlighted with lime green to make them look mossy, almost as if they belong in the middle of a forest.

Home sweet home.

Paint the shrubbery a couple of shades of green and use a smaller brush to change the color of any of the flowers in the garden beds or flowerpots.

Dig for Details

There are lots of details you can use to decorate your house that you may already have on hand, such as beads, broken jewelry parts, small gemstones, and pieces of mirror. Imagine what a fairy would collect: small, brightly colored items and anything shiny or glittery. Canvas your garden for dried seedpods, tiny cones, sheets of fallen bark, and interesting mossy twigs. Look for natural materials to use that you can take apart. For example, dried seed heads like allium consist of many smaller seed heads on tiny stems; look for the scales of a spruce or pine cone, or separate the individual petals of a dried hydrangea flower to add texture to a wall or door.

Add more flowers and make your own vines out of wire growing up the side of the wall, or glue some moss on the ivy to creep down from the windowsills. The wiring technique for the ivy is the same for both the house and the bench projects.

A tendency to overwork a fairy house comes with the territory of working in miniature. To prevent yourself from overdoing it or getting tunnel vision and only working on one part or one side of the house, step back from your work now and then to get a bigger picture of

A door fit for a fairy queen.

A mossy-looking thatched roof.

It's a fairy house; it doesn't have to make sense to us.

Layers of details add magic.

how the house looks. You want all four sides of the house to match or flow together. Repeat patterns and textures often, and keep the color palette consistent.

Small House, Big Garden

To make the garden more accessible for you (and your fairies), here are some pointers for planting a fairy house in a full-size garden bed:

1. Choose a spot where you will be comfortable working. Make sure there is a place in the garden for a stool to sit on and, this is also important, space to get back up without losing your balance or stepping on an accessory or plant by accident.

2. Leave a footpath for yourself to walk through your fairy garden. Include a few places in your garden design to walk in the fairy garden at a comfortable gait and places for you to stop to bend down. Playing the game Twister while trying to plant can get challenging.

3. Only show a part of the scene, or part of the fairy house, to tease the viewer to come in for a closer look. Letting the scene and the story unfold is more interesting than spreading out the whole scene in plain view.

4. The fairies in your garden don't have to be all in one spot. Fairies have wings and, word has it, they don't mind going over, around, through, or under

← Make the fairy paths big enough for you to walk on.

↓ Create a dramatic walkway up to the door just because you can.

the plants in the garden. They might have a nest in your full-size tree or perhaps a cocoon made of branches beside the front stoop for a daytime hideaway.

5. Separate your ideas into rooms. Create a garden room for each fairy idea rather than trying to arrange all the accessories into one area. Make the playgrounds separate from the eating area, for example.

6. Be sure to clear the yard for the fairies and make it neat with a walkway up to the front door. You can put up a small fence and make tiny garden beds in front of the house.

7. If your fairy furniture is not to scale with the house, place it away from the fairy house so the eye doesn't compare them, and then it won't be noticed.

8. Create a perimeter wall by using small branches that look like fallen logs. Nestle in small rocks that look like boulders with the bedding plants.

Planting a Fairy Haven

Once a spot for your fairy house is established, it's time to make it look as if fairies have been living in that spot forever. Plant three to five miniature trees and shrubs to instantly add age to the garden. This will help smooth the transition from the fairy house to your full-size garden. Using smaller plants and trees around the fairy house will provide layers that graduate from your regular garden down to fairy level.

LESS IS MORE

Focus on doing fewer things really well to create more of an impact. This idea resonates with all types of design, not just in the garden. The smartest-looking interiors are usually simply decorated with clean lines, patterns, and colors that are chosen for their strong presence.

Layer the trees and shrubs in the fairy bed as you would in your full-size garden.

You can redo the landscaping, too.

Just add (a little) fairy bling.

You can renovate an old fairy house or add personality to a new one.

PROJECT
FAIRY HOUSE REDUX

As you may already know, renovating a house is not an overnight task. Renovations take time, and whatever time frame the contractor quotes you, multiply it by 3.14. This project isn't as major as renovating a full-size house, but do take your time with this undertaking. Have fun tinkering with the fairy house but make sure each layer of paint and glue is dry before you move on to the next step. If you try to do everything at once and attempt to paint the freshly glued bits and pieces, it will get very messy.

In this project, you will be using an accelerant for superglues. This is a spray that dries any type of Crazy Glue (or cyanoacrylate adhesive) immediately upon contact. Use it in a well-ventilated area and follow the manufacturer's instructions. You can use it two ways: either apply glue to the house, place the object on the glue and then spray with the accelerant, or spray accelerant on the area where you want to place the object, put a drop of glue on the object, and place it where you sprayed accelerant. Be careful not to get accelerant on your hands because it's hard to remove. If you are prone to getting glue on your hands, buy some superglue remover or solvent; it will literally save your skin. You can wear gloves, but wearing gloves while you're working with miniatures often prevents you from feeling the tiny pieces, making it difficult to place them properly.

TOOLS AND MATERIALS

Fairy house

Paintbrushes, flat angle and small

Acrylic paint in white and other colors

Craft knife

Mirror tiles

Assorted decorations, such as beads, glitter, and jewelry parts

Drill with 1/16-inch bit

12- and 28-gauge colored wire, about 2 feet of each

Wire snips

Round-nose pliers

Scissors

Outdoor silicone glue

Crazy Glue

Accelerant for superglues

Paint tray

Metallic rub-on paint color

Mirror pieces or 1/4-inch tiles

Sealant

Clean, soft rag

INSTRUCTIONS

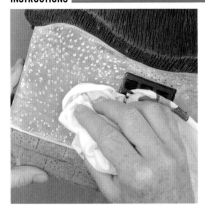

1 Begin with the walls of the house. Take advantage of any texture by painting the wall white (or a bright color) and gently wiping off the excess paint with a rag but keeping the color in the textured grooves. Let dry.

2 Using the flat brush, paint another color over the white base to highlight the textures. Let dry.

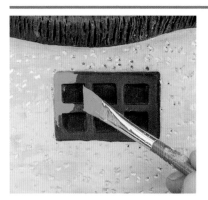

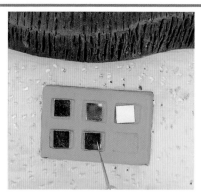

3 Paint the window frames. Let dry.

4 Working on one side of the house, adhere the mirror tiles onto each windowpane using silicone glue. Watch them until the glue sets to make sure the mirror pieces don't slide out of place. Use a craft knife to push them back into place if they do. Let dry. Then adhere the mirror tiles to the windows on the other sides of the house, letting them dry before moving on to a new side.

5 Working on one wall of the house at a time, glue the decorations onto the house. Let the glue dry. Then paint them white and let the paint dry. The base of white paint will make the second color even and more prominent.

6 Drill a few holes in the garden beds so you can do some landscaping with wire. Hold the drill lightly while drilling; you may break through the resin if you apply too much pressure. If you do break anything or make a mistake, rework the area by gluing on another object or two to disguise the error.

7 Create some fairy plants and ivy by twisting the different sizes of wire around the round-nose pliers to form tendrils. Install the wire tendrils by putting a drop of Crazy Glue in the hole, inserting a wire tendril, then squirting the hole with a spray of accelerant to dry the glue. Spray the entire house with sealant. Let dry. Plant the house in the fairy garden.

PROJECT
CUSTOMIZE A FAIRY BENCH

Match your fairy furniture to your fairy house by using the same colors and materials to customize both. Here, green wire is used as ivy on both the house and the chair. If the piece of furniture has a raised motif or other distinguishing feature, you can accentuate it with paint. For example, the leaves painted on the bench's backrest are highlighted with a metallic green wire that echoes the stems and veins in the leaf design.

TOOLS AND MATERIALS

Bench or other piece of furniture

Drill with ¹⁄₁₆-inch bit

12- to 28-gauge colored wire, including green to make ivy, about 2 feet of each

Wire snips

Round-nose pliers

Crazy Glue

Accelerant for superglues

Acrylic paint

Paintbrushes, angled, small, and large

Rub-on paint in a light or dark color

Sealant

Paint tray

↑ **You can reuse and re-fairy your faded fairy garden furniture to give it a second life.**

INSTRUCTIONS

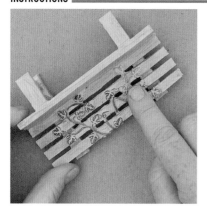

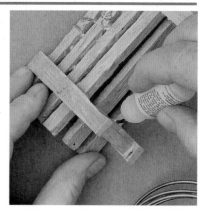

1 Using a paintbrush, paint the bench a base color. In this example, the base color is peach. If your piece of furniture has any raised details, use a light or dark rub-on paint on them to highlight them. If your base color is light, use a darker color; if your base color is dark, use a light color. Seal with sealant.

2 To mount the green ivy wire, drill a hole ¼ inch deep underneath the bench, in a corner where the leg of the bench meets the underside.

3 Insert the wire into the hole to make sure the hole is big enough and the right depth to hold the wire in place. If the hole isn't big enough, drill again. If the hole is the right size, squirt a small amount of Crazy Glue into the hole. Place the wire in the hole and spray a little accelerant on it. The glue will dry immediately.

Tiny flowers in matching colors are the icing on the fairy cake.

4 Using the round-nose pliers, grasp the wire and bend it into tendrils around the bench, bending it around the armrests, seat, and seatback in a design that you like. Be gentle while you're doing this, and try not to put too much pressure on the bench while bending the wire.

5 Add smaller tendrils of wire to help balance the bigger wire and to make it look less stark. Add more tendrils until your fairies are satisfied.

GNOME GARDEN

To paraphrase a famous movie line, *if you build it, they will come*: the gnomes, that is. No one will be able to resist this intriguing door nestled in a forest floor, especially not a gnome. With their encyclopedic knowledge of plants, birds, bugs, and weather, gnomes have been invading our imaginations since the sixteenth century. They appear in many forms, but they all seem to be small versions of us. So, what kind of miniature garden would a gnome enjoy tending? What would its home look like? Begin developing a gnome garden by thinking about your gnome's needs and personality.

Planting for Gnomes

The plant choices for this garden were chosen to conjure the edge of a forest. Use a lot of different greens, but be sure to mix up the size of the foliage so the plants do not blend together. In this project, the bushy lime-green 'Wilma Goldcrest' cypress is the perfect tree to anchor the back of the garden because it mimics a big forest tree. The miniature hostas help tell the scale of the garden, and they imitate large-leafed perennials. Irish moss and a few boulders tucked here and there simulate the edge of a field next to the forest and highlight

A birds-eye view of the gnome's garden.

the unique trunk structure on the 'Jervis' dwarf Canada hemlock. The vegetable bed is made with sedum cuttings. *Sedum spurium* has rosettes at the tips of the stems that can stand in for lettuce. The tricolor variety has a looser rosette in pink, cream, and green that mimics kale. Baby hens and chicks planted in rows look like miniature cabbages here.

Lumberjack Techniques

Gnomes are typically handy with tools, and Mother Nature's materials are plentiful, so a typical gnome's home would likely be made of materials found in the forest. Go on a scavenger hunt in your garden for supplies that you can use to build things. Bark, twigs, moss, leaves, seedpods, cones (pine, spruce, and deodora cones, for example), and stones can stand in for walls, boards, trim, and furniture parts for a gnome's home. The gnome door in this project is made with the stems from a common ninebark shrub that needs to be cut back each year to maintain its size. The fence is made from joe pye weed, a perennial wildflower. You will find some branches have a spongy interior, or pith, that will eventually dry and harden or slough off, leaving a tube-like twig as the outer layer hardens. These types of branches are fragile but great for splitting in two. Use the halves to make different designs or patterns for your gnome door. Older perennial branches are stiffer, and a stem from any perennial

A frolicking frog in miniature.

SUCCULENT CUTTINGS

When planting the succulent cuttings, either pinch them off the mother plant and put them aside for a couple of days before planting, or don't water them for a couple of days after planting. The end of the cutting needs to cauterize, or dry out, so the plant will know to root. If you plant the cutting and water it right away, the end will rot and the cutting will not take.

that you cut back every second year or third year will be harder and last longer on a project left outdoors. In general, annual stems tend to be very fragile and will decay quickly.

Small branches from trees and shrubs are ideal; branches from water sprouts and suckers are often straight. If you can, work with sturdier types of branches, but always experiment with them before you invest in doing a big project. You'll find that some branches crumble when you apply pressure to them, others are just too weak and delicate to work with, and some have bark that becomes brittle when dried. Keep in mind that anything fragile will not last long in the miniature garden, as it will repeatedly get wet, then dry out, and crumble from exposure to rain and moisture.

The branch or stem will shrink when it has dried out for a couple of days or weeks, depending on whether your climate is humid or dry. Always use dry, clean twigs for any glued project; adhesive will not work on damp or dirty material. Stems that range in diameter from $\frac{3}{16}$ to $\frac{1}{4}$ inch thick will make a suitable range of sizes for miniature fences.

An empty pail left behind in the vegetable bed starts the story.

A berm of Irish moss creates a subtle hillside, providing the perfect spot for nestling a gnome door.

PROJECT
DOOR TO A GNOME'S HOME

In this project, the stems are glued on with outdoor silicone glue that, when dry, remains shiny. The glue and the shine can be hidden with soil and leaves, so gather a small bowlful of garden scraps before you begin this project. You'll easily find soil bits, tiny fragments of leaves, chips of bark mulch, and moss scraps around your potting bench and garden bed. Sprinkle the mixture over the freshly glued branches, making sure it gets in between the stems, and it will look like the logs are naturally kept in place by a mud-like mortar.

A gnome door awaits.

TOOLS AND MATERIALS

4-inch nursery pot

Thirteen popsicle sticks

Sandpaper, fine grit

Heavy-duty scissors

Outdoor silicone glue

Dried twigs cut to these lengths: 12 twigs at 1½ inches long, 24 twigs at 3 inches long, and 12 twigs at 2 inches long

Bowl of garden scraps

Elastic band

Curly twig for the door handle

Preserved moss clump

Garden clippers

Paint tray

Acrylic paint in burnt umber

Paintbrush

Craft knife

Ruler

Soft, clean rag

INSTRUCTIONS

1 To make a base for the twigs to be glued to, hold the pot at the bottom and use the heavy-duty scissors to cut off the pot's side at a diagonal angle, making the shorter side less than 1½ inches high and the longer side less than 3 inches high. Cut the little nubs off the bottom of the pot to make a flush surface on which to glue the popsicle sticks.

2 Set the pot on a work surface with the bottom facing up. Starting at the center and working outward, use a popsicle stick to spread a layer of glue about ⅟₁₆ inch thick across the bottom of the pot. Place the popsicle sticks across the bottom of the pot, close together without any gaps in between. For the left and right sides of the pot, cut the popsicle sticks in half so that they don't overhang. Use a rag to clean up any glue that has oozed out. Let dry.

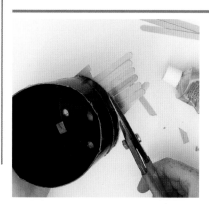

3 Using the heavy-duty scissors, cut off the overhanging ends of the sticks, working around the circumference of the pot. If there is any glue showing, sand it off with sandpaper, then sand the trimmed stick edges gently with sandpaper.

4 Starting on the longer side of the pot, which will be the top of the gnome door, spread some glue and begin placing the 3-inch-long twigs, aligning one end of each twig with the bottom of the pot so that the twig doesn't hang over. Place a few twigs at a time on the glue until about one-third of the pot is covered.

5 Sprinkle some garden scraps over the freshly glued sticks and use your fingers to work them gently into the crevices where the glue has oozed out.

6 Double-check that the sticks are aligned with the bottom of the pot by setting the pot bottom side down on a flat work surface. If the sticks are aligned with the bottom of the pot, it should sit flat on the work surface. If any sticks overhang, adjust them, then set the pot aside to dry. (Instead of adjusting the twigs one at a time, you can adjust all the sticks at once by putting a hand inside the pot and pressing the bottom of the pot against the flat work surface. The glue should still be wet at this point, so pressing the pot against the table will cause the twigs and pot to align.)

7 Repeat steps 4 through 6 using the shorter twigs on the shorter sides of the pot until the circumference of the pot is covered, letting the glue dry after each section is covered with twigs. Once the last section is covered with twigs and garden scraps, place a rubber band around the twigs to keep them in place and let the glue dry. Once the glue is dry, use the heavy-duty scissors to gently trim off the ends of the twigs to even them out around the cut side of the pot.

8 Mix a small amount of burnt umber paint with water to make a wash. Paint the front of the door and the tops of the twigs. Let dry.

9 Position a curly twig for the door handle on the door (trim it if necessary to make it sit flush on the door), then glue it to the door. Let dry. Use glue to tuck bits of moss in and around the door and the door handle. Let dry.

Try a variety of door handles, like differently shaped curly twigs or acorn tops.

PROJECT
LOG BORDER

This little log border is great for lining any garden bed because you can bend it anyway you like to conform to an angular or curvy garden bed and make it any length. In this project, you will use a jig, or template, as a guide so that you drill the holes in the branches the same distance apart. Keep the branches long; don't cut them before you drill or you won't have anything to hold on to. Always give yourself enough room to grip the piece if you are using a power drill. If the branches are too small to hold safely, err on the side of safety and use a vise or clamp instead of your fingers to hold them. Get a rhythm going and drill and cut both ends, then repeat, until you have enough pieces for a fence that fits your garden's edge.

If you want to make a long fence, consider using tree branches rather than perennial branches; they are stronger and stay intact while you're threading the wire through them. When making a circle, make two hooks in the wire at each end of the fence and hook them together to close the circle.

TOOLS AND MATERIALS

Piece of scrap wood

Ruler

Pen or marker

Dried branches, about 24 inches total, $\frac{3}{16}$ inch to ¼ inch thick

Drill with $\frac{1}{16}$-inch bit

Garden clippers

24-gauge wire, enough for the length of your fence

Wire cutters

Metal rod

Jewelry pliers

↑ The log fence separates the veggie garden from the moss-covered miniature field.

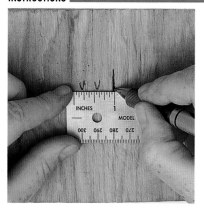

1 Mark a vertical line on the piece of scrap wood. This is the line that you'll position each twig next to. Measure and mark two notches beside it, one ⅜ inch from the first line and the other ¼ inch from the first notch.

2 Line up one end of a branch next to the first line you made. Drill a hole in the twig at the two noches that you marked. Line up the other end of the twig with the first line, and drill a hole in that end of the twig at the two noches that you marked. You should have four holes, two at each end of the twig.

3 Using the clippers, cut off each end of the twig just above the hole that's closest to the end of the twig. If you want a rustic-looking fence that's uneven across the top, vary the spot at which you cut the twig. If you want the fence to be level across the top, cut each twig the same distance from the end. (Mark the distance on the scrap wood and include that in the template.)

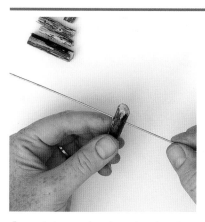

4 Using the jewelry pliers, bend each wire at a 90-degree angle about ⅜ inch from the end. This will help keep the first twig from falling off the end of the wires. Thread the wire through the first twig and line up the wire for the rest.

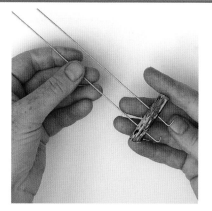

5 Be forgiving as you thread the pieces onto the wire because the wire may twist as you put the pieces on. Gently line them back up by keeping one of your fingers in between them while threading the wire through the logs. You may have to twist the logs to make them even up. Remember to be gentle if you are using delicate twigs.

6 Go over the line of branches once they are all on and push them against the bent end of the wire and against one another so you do not see any space between them.

7 Bend the other ends of the wires 90 degrees to hold the branches in place. Leaving enough bent wire to hold the twigs in place, snip off the excess wire.

8 Push a metal rod into the branches at each end of the fence to stake the fence upright in the soil. If you're using hard wood or thick branches, you may have to drill a hole in the bottom of the two end twigs to stake them.

9 Bend the fence into a curved shape, make a sharp corner, or leave it straight. Insert in your garden. Whew! It's a lot more fun to build a miniature fence than a full-size fence, isn't it?

A basket of miniature acorns waits by the gnome door.

DESERTED ISLAND SURVIVAL

Have you ever imagined being stranded on a deserted island? Do you enjoy the old island adventure books and movies, *Swiss Family Robinson* or *Robinson Crusoe*? If so, you can now have your own island paradise to call home anytime you like. There's no guarantee you will meet anyone named Friday or Gilligan, and it may involve a wild boar or a monkey or two, but it will be your own island.

The classic voyage-and-return story line has captivated our imagination in countless movies and novels. The hero ends up stranded on a strange island, overcomes his fears and, in the end, succeeds either by being rescued or by being resourceful and making the best of the situation until rescuers arrive. This garden can be the beginning of your own (imaginary) adventure story. You can set the scene in your own tiny jungle and begin to fill in the details. This isn't just a one-and-done mission either. You need to survive until you can find a way off the island, and your first chore is to make some shelter.

An unpruned hinoki cypress tree, rescued from an old miniature garden, provided an ideal perch for this tree house.

Gimme Shelter

A miniature tree house suspended among the branches in a tropical paradise with a tiny pet monkey is an exciting idea that teases you with its potential for whimsy. A multilevel tree-top estate with huts perched in the branches, linked together with bridges, platforms, and ladders is enough to capture anyone's imagination, but to miniaturize all those juicy details and make the buildings weatherproof and durable is an undertaking that may take months to complete. The goal here is to construct a simple house that is sturdy enough so that it stays in the tree.

Planting a Deserted Island

The idea for this garden came from an unpruned hinoki cypress tree that was salvaged from an old miniature garden. The tree was still happily growing, but only from the topmost branches, which made the cypress look like a really tall palm tree. The spindly branches just beckoned for a tree house. The plants that make up the understory have a similar otherworldly and tropical sensibility. The 'Whipcord' western red cedar's large threadlike foliage looks almost prehistoric and is ideal for sheltering a small cave. Planted a bit sideways, a wind-damaged dwarf spruce tree was perfect for the side of the riverbed. And the grassy plant is dwarf chives, with stems that stiffen up and turn darker green when the weather warms up for spring. Small hens and chicks with red and green leaves help fill in the understory, adding structure and interest.

Use plants that have a tropical look. An unpruned hinoki cypress stands in for a palm tree here.

The strips of wood used to build this tree house look like they may have washed up on shore. The roof is slanted to prevent rainwater from pooling on it.

Tree house materials

You can find strips of wood for the tree house at hobby stores in the model railroad section or in craft stores in the unfinished wood section. Most of the wood you'll find will be soft balsa wood, but you'll be treating it for outdoor use with a wood hardener. Professional woodshops usually have a scrap bin with long strips of different kinds of wood in a range of thicknesses and sizes. If you have your own wood workshop, you'll likely have a lot of scrap wood on hand.

You'll also need a block of wood for this project; if you don't have one lying around in your garage, perhaps a neighbor will. Some hardware stores that offer custom woodcutting will have a scrap bin; you might find some wood that's the right size there. Get a couple of different sizes and shapes so you can test how the block will sit in the tree before you decorate it.

Scale

There is no particular scale used in this miniature garden project. The tree house will dictate the scale of the garden, making this project even more fun because you don't have to do any measuring. The beauty of making all the accessories for a deserted island garden, or any miniature garden, is that you can make them any size you like (because the plants and trees can be viewed differently). For example, a small shrub can appear to be a big tree if there is a tiny cave underneath it. This spindly cypress appears to be an enormous tropical tree with a tiny tree house in it. Start by making a door that's in proportion with the block of wood, and then you will know what size to make the window frames, the cave, and whatever else you may need on an island, like a raft, a bridge, or furniture.

BUILD A LADDER TO THE STARS

You'll need a way to reach your tree house. A knotted climbing rope is easy to make, and regular cotton string is the perfect size for a miniature rope; just tie knots along the string at an equal distance apart, then tie it to the branch where the tree house will sit. If the perch for the tree house is closer to the ground, a rope ladder may look more appropriate. You can make a rope ladder from branches and rope, or weave one with just rope, a very doable task in miniature. You can find larger rope ladders or net ladders at stores that specialize in pet birds and accessories for their cages.

A rope ladder provides access to the tree house.

PROJECT
TREE HOUSE

The tree house starts with a small block of wood. If it falls out of your tree, it won't break easily. The more the little house weathers and ages naturally, the better it will look. You can nestle it in the tree canopy or secure it to a branch with wire.

The tree that you choose for your tree house will dictate the size of the block of wood that you need. Don't overload the branches with a big block; keep it small because you may want a balcony around the sides. The block of wood shown in this project is a 2-inch piece cut from the end of a 2 × 4, making it the perfect size for this tree.

Some tree houses will fit naturally in the tree canopy, while others may need a little help to stay put. A bushier canopy will be able to hold the tree house in place without any additional wiring, but in a leggy tree the house may need to be wired in place to stay nestled among the branches. Hammer a small brad nail into the back of the house to attach a wire to it.

Use this building technique to make a big fort or garden shed for another spot in your miniature garden. The only caveat is to stay away from a small square-shaped house or it may look like an outhouse (unless that's the look you're after). The glue used in this project is an all-purpose heavy-duty silicone glue applied thinly with a popsicle stick.

↑ **A makeshift tree house fashioned out of strips of wood shelters castaways in this deserted island garden.**

TOOLS AND MATERIALS

Wood block, about 2 × 2 × 4 inches

Wood strips

Craft knife

Cutting mat

Ruler

Scissors

Silicone glue

Popsicle stick for spreading glue

Paintbrush

Acrylic paint in Payne's gray or burnt umber

Water

Paverpol

Clean, soft rag

Small nail, optional, to attach the tree house to wire

28-gauge wire, optional, to attach the tree house to a branch

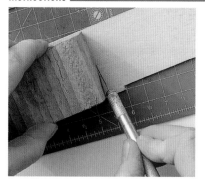

1 Use the block of wood to measure and score the piece of wood for the roof where you want to cut it. Working on the cutting mat, use the ruler as a straight edge and cut the piece of wood for the rooftop along the scored lines.

2 Go through your pieces of wood and cut enough panels to cover all four sides of the wood block. Then, slice some narrow strips of wood to use for the door and window frames to glue on in step 3; and cut those in proportion to the block of wood. Cut three narrow strips of wood to use as supports for the deck. They should be approximately ½ inch deeper that the block of wood so that they can extend out from underneath the house and support the deck.

3 Glue the panels on the block of wood. Let dry. Before gluing on the rooftop, glue a strip of wood underneath the roof, along the edge that will be the back of the roof. This strip will make the roof slant toward the front. Glue on the rooftop piece. Add roof extensions to provide protection from rain by gluing a narrow piece of wood onto each end of the roof. Glue on the strips of wood for the door and window frames. Glue on any other embellishments. Let dry.

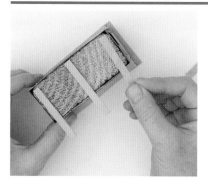

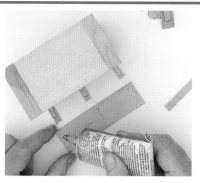

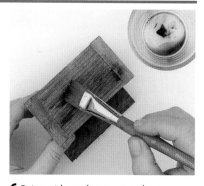

4 Glue the three strips of wood for the deck onto the bottom of the block of wood. Let dry.

5 Line up the deck with the three support pieces so that you know where to put the glue, and glue the deck on top of the support pieces. Let dry.

6 Paint with washes to give the tree house an aged appearance. Let dry. To weatherproof the shelter, apply a coat of Paverpol on all sides of the tree house. Gently tack a tiny nail to the bottom of the house, or on the backside. Don't hammer the nail all the way into the house; leave about ¹⁄₁₆ inch of the nail exposed to attach a wire that can be fastened around the tree's branch. Install the tree house in the tree and attach the rope ladder to a nearby branch.

PROJECT
MAKE A CAVE

The black nursery pot used in this project is 2 inches in diameter. Use a bigger pot if you want a bigger cave, of course, but divide the gluing steps into two or three sessions, and let the glue dry after each session. (Gluing the pieces together all at once will end up in a big mess.) Try to find black nursery pots, as the pot tends to show through despite how well covered it is with pebbles and sand. If you don't have your own stack of nursery pots from your own gardening exploits, ask any gardener for one or find some used ones at a garden center. You can buy a new plastic pot for this project, but you'll be cutting it up and gluing onto it.

TOOLS AND MATERIALS

Small nursery pot

Scissors

Silicone glue

Popsicle stick for spreading glue

Small pebbles collected in a tray or dish

Superfine sand collected in a tray or dish

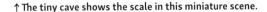
↑ The tiny cave shows the scale in this miniature scene.

1 Cut the nursery pot almost in half at a diagonal angle. Trim the edges to make sure the cut edge is straight and sits flush on a flat work surface.

2 Squirt some silicone glue onto the pot and use the stick to spread the glue, covering half of the outside of the nursery pot with glue, then press the pot into the tray of pebbles. Use your fingers to rearrange or add pebbles and fill in any gaps.

3 Press the pebbles down gently so they stick into the glue.

4 While the glue is still wet, sprinkle sand over and in between the pebbles. Let dry. Repeat steps 2 through 4 to finish covering the pot with the pebbles and sand. Install the cave in the garden. Light fire. Cook food.

You may not mind being stranded on this deserted island.

COLONIZING OUTER SPACE

Okay, this is a project where you can truly let your freak flag fly because this is an opportunity to create a planet and alien species far, far from Earth. Lock the hatches and engage the engines; your journey to another planet is about to begin.

One of the many things that miniature gardening has done is to change the way we view plants. For example, a young shrub is no longer just a shrub but a potential tree in a miniature garden. Hold it up at eye level and look directly at it to envision the tiny landscape around it. Look under its foliage to see what kind of trunk and branching pattern it has, and consider how it would look as a tree in your miniature garden. Some plants have a growth habit that, if left unchecked to grow into a leggy shrub, can look completely alien but ideal for a plant in an outer space–themed garden.

Containing Outer Space

Putting all seriousness aside, let's discuss choosing a container for your planet. For this garden, an old satellite dish fit the theme perfectly because it looks like a flying saucer. A wide saucer keeps the garden balanced and corrals any excess water, and its shallow depth is

Houston, we've made contact! Succulents and a customized pine cone give this garden the aura of an alien landscape.

ideal for a dry dish garden because succulent roots do not need a lot of space. Other examples of out-of-this-world containers for an outer-space garden can be found in not-so-ordinary places. Look for weird and wonderful ideas in secondhand-goods stores and recycling centers. The plumbing and electrical departments in hardware stores have small-scale items, like a small electrical junction box or PVC caps that can be transformed into something weird and wonderful. Just about anything painted any shade of gray or silver will deliver a spaceship spirit, including metal trays, hollowed-out monitors, old tires, or perhaps a discarded hubcap.

Remember that a garden in a container that does not have a drainage hole will need closer monitoring than a garden in a container with drainage holes because excess water can't escape and may drown the plants. The satellite dish in this project has a couple of small mounting holes to provide adequate drainage for a dry succulent garden. If you don't want your container to have any drainage holes, then follow the same rules for planting and caring for your garden as you would for dish gardening.

Planting Outer Space

This project started off with a large purple aeonium that had become a little leggy. With its bare trunk and stem and pom-pom foliage, the plant makes a terrific alien-looking plant. The rest of the plant choices followed easily, and the succulent family became the perfect

Take me to your leader. Small cones make excellent heads or bodies for an alien species.

Succulents that are in the middle of propagating make the best alien plants if you can resist taking cuttings from the mother plant for as long as possible.

stand-in for a far-away planet's landscape. The rigid, geometric structure of their leaves, the wild color combinations, and the extraterrestrial quality of their growth habit when left alone were all considerations but, more important, it is their compatibility with the aeonium, the plant that started it all, that makes them so ideal for an outer-space garden. All the plants in this garden thrive indoors in bright light and dry soil.

Arrange the plants randomly around the planter to make it look like they are colonizing naturally. In this garden, vermiculite was used for decorative mulch. Try to find strange-looking items to embellish the landscape such as small lava rocks, dried roots, or oddly shaped cones. In this project, shell-covered rocks were placed in groups, all facing the same direction, to look like alien pods. (Don't knock an alien invasion; it could really happen one day!)

Spawn an Alien Race

Creating an alien race may sound daunting because there's no real reference point to work from. You are creating a life form from scratch, so where do you start? When you come up against a question like this, look to where it's been done before: Hollywood. The film and television industry regularly comes up with versions of aliens, many of which are hilariously fake looking. But an Internet search will get your sci-fi inspiration going. While you're looking at images, pay attention to the individual characteristics that attract you, such as eye shape, quirky body structure, and pointy ears, for example. Make a note of them for your own aliens: they'll give you something to start with.

Another way into creating an alien species is leaving it up to nature. Plant life makes great alien life, so you'll find endless material in your garden to make endearingly wacky aliens from. A banksia pod alone can be an extraterrestrial being. Cones, seedpods, seashells, branches, stripped-down flower stems, and leaves can be taken apart or joined together to make small and large creatures. Add color and the colonization of your planet can begin. The following project shows you how to make cute aliens out of cones, branches, and little bit of paint.

'Calico Kitten' crassula reaching for light. A collection of shell-covered rocks found at a garage sale made the perfect pods for this new colony.

Miniature succulent gardens are a great place to get a
few cuttings started for other garden projects.

PROJECT
MAKE AN ALIEN

You will need two things to make your aliens come alive: personality and animation. For personality, work a human element onto the creatures. Instead of just a blob, define a head somehow. It can be any shape or size, as long as you differentiate the head, or heads, from the body. Go back to your Internet search on Hollywood's aliens and you'll notice that the most popular aliens, like E.T., have a human quality.

To animate the aliens, make arms or legs for them; even if the aliens are standing still, arms and legs will give them an endearing appearance. People will be able to relate to an alien if they can see a part of themselves in it. In this project, white oak acorn caps make up the body and the head of the aliens. Tiny branches from the trimmings of a thyme-leaf cotoneaster make perfect legs (or arms, if you like) for the creatures.

↑ A simple yet alien creature.

TOOLS AND MATERIALS

White oak acorn caps

Twigs

Acrylic paint in assorted colors

Paint tray

Paintbrush

Wire clippers

Hot-glue gun

Paverpol

INSTRUCTIONS

1 Determine what colors you would like the twigs (legs) and acorn caps (heads) to be, then paint them. Let dry.

2 Mix and match the acorn caps and twigs together to see how you would like them to fit, then clip the twigs to the desired length if necessary.

3 Hot-glue dries quickly, so arrange the pieces of your alien creature in front of you so that you can put them together before the glue dries. Then, using a hot-glue gun, fill an acorn cap with glue.

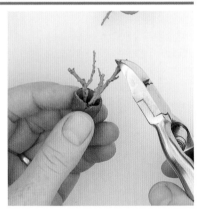

4 Arrange the twig legs in the cap before the glue cools. If you need to reheat the glue, touch the tip of the hot-glue gun on the spots you want to remelt and rearrange the twig quickly. Let the glue cool. Repeat with the remaining acorn caps and twig legs.

5 Test how the aliens stand up on their twig legs and, if necessary, adjust the length of the legs by snipping them with wire clippers a little at a time until they stand the way you would like them to. Use a paintbrush to gently coat the aliens in Paverpol to weatherproof them. Let dry. Now choose your alien leader to begin the negotiation with the humanoids.

PROJECT
THE MOTHERSHIP

Mother Nature offers the best miniature parts on the planet for making spaceships. If you look closely at the wide variety of seedpods that nature produces, not to mention all the other flora, you will start to believe that perhaps we are the aliens. It's fun to scavenge for spaceship-worthy materials, not to mention inexpensive if you don't count the gas and the picnic. Before heading out, check your local laws regarding scavenging on public land and don't scavenge on private land without permission from the owner.

Seedpods and cones of all shapes and sizes can be a piece of a spaceship, or a spaceship in its entirety. Gather more materials than you think you'll need so that you can arrange and rearrange the pieces to see what fits together well. Make sure your base balances the spaceship, you'll want to be sure that a top-heavy accessory will stand up properly. Stake the spaceship afterward to help it stand upright in the garden bed. Make sure all the materials are fully dried before you start. You can use hot-glue on it because you are gluing inside the cone and the glue won't be exposed to the elements. If you are parking your spaceship outside, treat it with UV-protectant spray.

If a door opens, start running.

COLONIZING OUTER SPACE | 189

TOOLS AND MATERIALS

Assorted cones and seed pods, including one large cone

Linesman's pliers

Drill with ¹⁄₁₆-inch bit

Leather gloves (optional)

Hot-glue gun

Paintbrush

Two metal rods, ¹⁄₁₆ inch thick and about 8 inches long

Metallic spray paint

Scissors

UV-protectant spray

INSTRUCTIONS

1 Snip the end off the base of the large cone to make a flat surface to drill into.

2 Wear leather gloves for this step if you like, to help protect your hand if the drill slips. Drill a hole in the base of the large cone. Hold the cone delicately but firmly; if you grip it too hard, you may break the scales of the cone. Be alert to how you are holding the cone when you drill to avoid placing your hand in the path of the drill bit.

3 Using the paintbrush, clean the cone, brushing in between the scales to clean out any dirt or sawdust.

4 Repeat steps 1 through 3 with all the other cones and the seedpods. If possible, drill the smaller cones all the way through the middle; you'll need to push a metal rod through them in step 9.

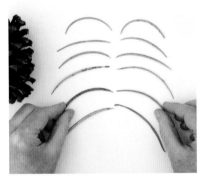

5 Decorate your spaceship. Try to embellish the spaceship all the way around for the best effect, so that it looks good from every side. Take advantage of symmetry possibilities wherever you can.

6 To glue material deep inside the cone, use the hot-glue gun and work on one spot at a time. Insert the nozzle into the middle of the cone, place the material in the hot glue, and hold it in place until the glue cools.

7 Strip the scales off one seedpod and glue them to another seedpod to make a rocket booster.

8 Tack the scales onto the cone with a little bit of hot glue, then reinforce the cone from underneath with more hot glue to strengthen the join.

9 Assemble the ship on the metal rod. It will hold the pieces together and act as a stake to keep the spaceship upright in the garden. Insert the rod through the hole that was drilled in the cones. Arrange and rearrange them on the rod until they're in an order that you like. Then, working on one cone at a time, put small dabs of glue between cones to glue them together, using the rod to help keep the pieces together.

10 If the rod isn't long enough to be used as a stake for the ship, drill into the bottom of the ship and glue in another rod.

11 Spray the spaceship silver. Let dry. Spray with UV-protectant spray if it will be outdoors. Now give it to your aliens, they are waiting for it.

UNDER THE SEA

A fish tank is a world within a world that instantly adds a calm, quiet, and peaceful atmosphere to any room. Aquariums require a lot of maintenance and a lot of water changes and, as the saying goes, you need to love getting your sleeves wet. So, how's this for a little change: a miniature garden that looks like it's the bottom of the sea floor.

Creating a sea floor requires more collecting than designing, so call on your inner Nemo, toss out the usual garden design rules, and go get your shell collection because you now have a place to display it. All you need is a little imagination and a love of the sea.

If you don't have a shell collection, then head to the beach. Or, head to a craft store. You can still tell people that you collected the shells personally, just skip the part about going to a craft store to collect them. You can also find all kinds of exotic shells, coral, urchins, and starfish online.

If you collect the shells at the beach and want to use them in your miniature garden right away, boil them for 15 to 20 minutes to leech out some of the salt and kill any remaining organic debris. If you're using store-bought shells, ask the clerk if they need to be boiled, or boil them anyway to be on the safe side. When working in small scales such as this, there are seldom any issues of the salt leaching into the garden soil or the plant's roots.

As the Beatles put it, "I'd like to be under the sea."

Planting Atlantis

Once you decide where you'll place your garden, narrow down your plant choices by focusing on strange-looking plants but keep in mind that their water and light needs must be compatible. Look for plants with foliage that has a sea-like texture, and choose patterns that you might find at the bottom of the sea. Mix up the sizes of the foliage and don't be afraid to include colorful leaves in the mix; the colors of the fish and foliage in the ocean range from neons to neutrals.

In this example, the very fine leaves of the miniature hebe look like bubbles, the needle-like bursts on the ends of the branches of the 'Slowmound' mugo pine are reminiscent of clusters of coral, and with its feather-like leaves and unchecked leggy growth 'Angelina' sedum looks like kelp. The plant textures contribute to the underwater feel, but it's the seashells and the accessories that cinch the theme. Using a layer of seashells on top of the soil for mulch slows down water evaporation from the soil. If you are using drought-tolerant plants, as in this example, their water needs are greatly reduced with a layer of seashell mulch.

Leave some areas in your underwater landscape free of plants and shells, and remember that this is not a conventional garden design but rather a sea floor, so plant at whim. Make different levels if you can. In this project, pieces from a pot similar to the outer container were used to elevate the main seating area, which gave the trough at the front of the pot more character.

The accessories and accents help plants morph into an underwater world.

Barnacles, shells, coral pieces, and like-colored
stones help deliver the theme.

Lovely thrones await for the monarchs of the undersea world.

PROJECT
GLASS FLOAT

A glass float, netted in knotted thread, adds a bit of shimmer under the sea.

TOOLS AND MATERIALS

Corkboard or sturdy cardboard

Straight pins

Sheet of lined paper

Scissors

Ruler

Heavy thread

Glass marble

A miniature glass float sparkles in the seabed.

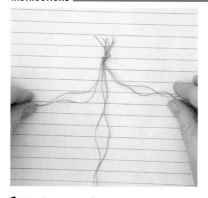

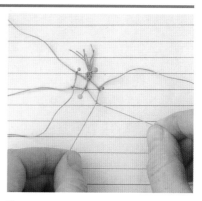

1 Pin the piece of paper to the cork-board. Cut 6 lengths of thread at least 8 inches long. This will give you long lengths of thread to work with; then you'll cut off the excess in step 5. Tie the ends of all 6 lengths together into an overhand knot and pin the knot to the corkboard, aligning the knot with a line on the paper. Separate the threads into three sets of two strands each, one set at left, one set in the middle, and one set at the right.

2 Using the two middle threads, make a square knot, aligning it at the next line on the paper. If you hold the strings taut, you will have more control of the placement of the knot. Repeat for the other two pairs of threads, giving you three square knots in a row. Pin the two outside knots to the paper and align them with the lines on the paper to keep track of them.

3 For the next row, take the right-hand thread from the middle pair of threads and the left-hand thread from the pair at the right, and make a square knot with them that aligns at the next line on the paper. Repeat, using the left thread from the middle pair and the right thread from the pair at the left. For the final knot, you will have to move the knotted piece around in order to join them to make the net bowl-shaped to hold the marble. Tie the third square knot on this row, lining it up with other knots to keep it even.

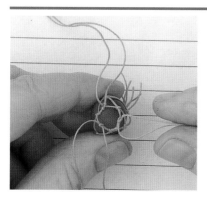

4 Fit the marble in the netting, gather up the loose ends, and tie another over-hand knot snugly against the bottom of the marble.

5 Braid about 1 inch of the loose ends together, and tie one last knot at the end of the braid to tie the ends together. Cut off the threads below the final knot to create the tassel. Remember to check all netting and floats after each fishing expedition, to keep them in tip-top shape and ready to go.

A throne fit for Poseidon, in
miniature, of course.

PROJECT
SEA THRONE

Making furniture for an undersea garden calls for a fair amount of whimsy. Depending upon the shells you're working with, you may have to glue together objects that don't fit together well, so you'll need to disguise the glue that holds the items together. In this example, round olive shells are glued to a round clamshell bottom to give the throne legs, inevitably leaving glue exposed where the two pieces are joined. Hide the exposed glue by sprinkling sand or moss on the wet glue just after gluing the pieces together.

Give the throne's backrest more character by extending a line of mossy bling to the top of the shell. Poke some beads and sparkles into the moss, and glue a tiny mirror to the backrest to make it look like it has a window.

The decorations used on the clamshell throne were found in various places. The tubes of tiny gemstones and beads came from a garage sale, the micro beads were found at a miniature store, and the tiny mirrors were taken from a placemat. You can find more tidbits to add to the throne by taking apart holiday ornaments, floral decorations, artificial flower sprays, or costume jewelry. You'll be able to find bags of shells at a craft store. To add a bit of magic, include at least one sparkly embellishment that will catch the eye and twinkle for the viewer.

TOOLS AND MATERIALS

Three small oval-shaped shells, olive shells, or small cowrie shells, about ¾ inch long

Large clamshell, about 3 inches wide

Silicone glue

Superfine sand

Ruler

Small piece of cardboard

Scissors

Small fabric swatch with small pattern

Aleene's Fast Grab Tacky Glue or craft glue

Model railroad turf

Small decorations such as beads, tiny mirror tiles, small gemstones, or rhinestones

Thin metal rod or skewer

Tweezers

INSTRUCTIONS

1 Arrange and rearrange the flat side of the three olive shells to see how they will fit on the bottom of the clamshell and hold it upright like a chair. Once you've determined an arrangement that will be stable, glue the flattest side of each olive shell onto the bottom of the clamshell. You'll have the most success when the silicone glue has been left to dry to a tacky state before joining both pieces. For example, dab some glue onto the flattest side of each olive shell and onto the bottom of the clamshell where you want it glued, but let the glue dry about 5 minutes, then attach the olive shells to the clamshell.

2 Make sure the clamshell sits level on its new feet on a flat work surface before the glue dries completely; adjust the olive shells if necessary. Once you're satisfied, sprinkle sand on the still-wet glue to hide it. Let dry. The join should dry in about an hour, but be sure to check the glue manufacturer's directions, too.

3 At the inside bottom of the clamshell, measure the distance from one side to the other and cut an oval piece of cardboard to fit. This will be the seat cushion for the throne.

4 Place the fabric swatch pattern side down on your work surface, and place the cardboard oval on top of the fabric. Cut the fabric swatch so that it is about ¾ inch larger than the oval around all sides. Fold an edge of the fabric over the cardboard, apply some Tacky Glue to the cardboard and the top of the folded-over fabric, and fold another piece of fabric over the cardboard onto the glue. Working a little bit at a time, repeat around the oval until all the fabric is glued on. Let the cushion dry completely.

5 Apply a ring of Tacky Glue to the clamshell where the cushion will touch the clamshell. Place the cushion.

6 Hold the chair with one hand, and using the tweezers, carefully place tiny bits of the turf in the crevices in between the cushion and the shell where the glue is seeping out. Use the metal rod to position the gemstones and beads in the glue around the oval seat until you have a design that you like.

7 Apply a line of Tacky Glue up the backrest of the throne and use the metal rod to place moss, beads, and a mirror on the glue in a design that you like.

8 Finish decorating the throne by tucking tiny bits of the light green moss here and there to soften up the seating area. Get your kelp crown on, grab your scepter, and have a seat.

Keep swimming.

BEYOND THE MINIATURE GARDEN

WARDIAN CASE

A Miniature Atrium

Atriums have become the most popular room in the house for gardeners of all kinds, and it's unfortunate that most houses don't have one. Who doesn't love a glass room that makes you feel like you are outdoors even on the coldest day of winter? It's a room where plants are a must, daylight reaches every corner, and the atmosphere feels like a tropical vacation. Well, you can have all this in miniature.

This project transforms a Wardian case into a miniature atrium. Enjoy it as a focal point for meditation in your yoga room, keep it next to your favorite chair in the living room for daydreaming, or put it in the office waiting room; it's perfect for wherever a little space to dream is needed.

Wardian cases make excellent miniature atriums because they are ready-made, can withstand moisture from the plants, and are easy to maintain. The difference between a Wardian case and a terrarium is in the way in which plants are grown in them. Both house tiny plants, are usually tabletop-size, and can fit only a few small plants, but the plants in a Wardian case are in pots, whereas in a terrarium the plants are planted in soil right

in the terrarium; in other words, the terrarium is the pot. There is a little overlap with Wardian cases nowadays, and many are marketed as terrariums, but terrariums are watertight and Wardian cases are usually not.

Planting an Atrium

Having a contained room such as a miniature atrium opens up another way to grow tiny plants that need a little more care than regular houseplants. Plants like ferns, African violets, and miniature begonias draw moisture from the air as well as through their roots and do very well in an enclosed environment. Peperomias, baby tears, small-leafed coleus, and pileas are all plants with similar needs and perfect for a Wardian case; they don't mind the humidity at their roots and leaves. Do not try to populate a Wardian case with any outdoor miniature garden plants; they will not like the contained environment. When in doubt, research a plant's needs before placing it in a Wardian case.

In this example, ponytail palms anchor the two back corners. The pots in the front right corner are planted with tillandsias (air plants), and the tiny potted garden is planted with sedum cuttings, which will last a month or two before needing to be replaced.

Mimic your own decor or create your dream room.

A miniature room that you
can rearrange at will.

Make sure your accessories are in proportion to the height of the room.

Sizing Up Your Atrium

Size up your Wardian case to see what scale works best for it and follow the same rules for assessing a pot for miniature gardening. If the Wardian case is 10 inches or larger on any side, use large-size or 1-inch scale accessories. If it is less than 10 inches on all sides, use medium-size accessories or ½-inch scale accessories. It may be easier to find plants for larger-scale Wardian cases.

Don your dollhouse cap and choose a style of Wardian case that reflects the theme you want to carry throughout the room. For example, in this project, the arched windows evoke a modern Victorian feeling, so the bright color of the classic settee and table is appropriate. Other styles of Wardian cases echo high Victorian; medieval; goth; English garden; old-fashioned country; and modern-country themes. There are geometric and artistic glass cases that look very stylish and would suit a fun 1970s retro-style garden or a space-age garden room.

Cleaning Your Atrium

To maintain the plants in the atrium, remove them to water them, and let the water drain before returning the plants to the atrium. Even though this atrium has a pebble floor to lift the pots off the floor of the atrium, try to keep water out of the atrium as much as possible. If you keep the lid open for long periods of time dust will accumulate inside, of course, so you'll need to clean out the room now and then. Otherwise the atrium shouldn't require much cleaning, except to dust the top of the lid of the case. Don't you wish all housekeeping could be this easy?

There is room for a little fun with the different sizes of plants.

PROJECT
YOUR OWN MINIATURE ATRIUM

Large-size accessories, small potted plants, and a few accents will make this miniature atrium cozy and inviting. This is an opportunity to tap into your inner interior designer and decorate a room exactly the way you have always wanted to.

Do you love lace curtains but your husband doesn't? Are you fond of the color pink but have yet to convince your family members to paint the living room a dusty rose color? Do you secretly admire sleek, modern furniture but have a craftsman-style house? Designing a room for a Wardian case allows you to decorate to your heart's content, get the feeling of working with a dollhouse without all the work, and realize the garden room of your dreams, in miniature.

First, define the purpose of the room because this will influence the focal point. Do you want one chair just for you to visually sit on with a little table for a book? Do you want a couch to lie down on or space to invite a guest to sit for tea? Think about the story you want to tell; it will give you a direction to begin with.

In the example, the focal point is the couch and seating area. Once you've envisioned those furnishings, you can decorate the room like any full-size room. Choose a matching rug, consider window treatments, shop for the couch, and figure out the size and shape of the plants you need. Here, a pair of small ponytail palms suited the corners perfectly, and the arch of their grassy foliage mimics the window arches.

A sculpture of Summer stands in one front corner of the atrium. The statue is interesting on all four sides, so we don't mind seeing the side or back of her on occasion through the Wardian case. Smaller details like the mini-mini garden, the animal statues, and the book on the table lure the viewer in for a closer look. Keep the room simple and uncluttered; remember that in design, less is more.

← A bird's-eye view of a decorated Wardian case.

↑ Tea for two?

There is always room for a miniature garden.

1 Place a layer of pebbles in the Wardian case. Use something flat to tamp down the pebbles and settle them into the bottom.

2 Position the carpet and resist the urge to put it dead center in the room; place it slightly off center for more interest. Here, the carpet is closer to the back of the Wardian case than to the front.

3 Start with your focal point and work out from there. The focal point in this room is the settee and table.

4 Finish with the plants, statue, and details.

5 You are welcome here anytime.

BROKEN-POT GARDENING

Creating a fairy garden in a broken pot has become popular in recent years. Perhaps it's because there are a large number of broken pots available, or perhaps it's because the idea is a really creative one that works perfectly with any fairy theme. But these types of fairy gardens are temporary at best because the pot-pieces tend to fall away as soon as the roots start growing, the gardens are hard to water in the dry months. Be careful if you try to move it; it will be off balance and may fall apart.

Use this idea to make a miniature broken-pot garden that holds together for more than a few months, is easier to water and maintain, and looks more cohesive than a jumble of pot shards, succulents, and a little house. The broken-pot idea simply looks better when a lot of plants are used rather than it being merely a stage for fairy houses and accessories. A broken-pot design looks best when it is simplified because it can quickly look cluttered when there are too many pot shards and too many accessories being used. Again, less is more, and there is something magical and endearing in keeping it simple.

Using a broken pot to plant in changes the rules for container gardening. Once a container is cracked or broken, the environment for the plant's roots is compromised. What was once a contained environment that could retain moisture in the soil and shield roots from light is now an exposed environment that can dry out unexpectedly. But by using the right plants and treating this idea a little bit differently, you can make a long-lasting garden in a broken pot.

While there are many photographs of broken-pot gardens on the Internet, what you don't see are photographs that reflect the results after many years of growing. This is because most of the pots are overplanted, and the photograph is often taken shortly after the garden has been put together, so it looks its best.

Parched Popularity

A popular pot for broken-pot fairy gardens is terra-cotta, which is a porous material and wicks moisture out of the soil and away from the plant's roots. A glazed pot is a much better container to start with and it doesn't have to be broken either; you can break it the way you want.

Find a broken pot at your local garden center; with luck you won't have to pay for it because it really is unsellable. If the nursery is creating their own broken-pot gardens and charging for them, you probably will have to pay for it. If this is the case, then you may as well get a pot that you really like and break it yourself, instead of compromising with someone else's seconds.

A broken pot offers an opportunity for additional areas to plant in.

A tiny sedum cutting in a pot can help
tell the scale of the garden.

Plants from left to right: golden baby tears, Lawson's cypress, Corsican mint, and Irish moss in front.

If you are on a budget, look for chipped or cracked pots at the store and see if you can negotiate for a better price. First make sure the chip can be hidden, or follow the crack to see if it's going to break in the right way for your idea. Also look for pots with gaps in the glaze or some sort of kiln damage or irregularity in the paint. These kinds of pots are often the last to be sold, so the retailer might welcome the negotiation.

Ring of Truth

This technique for finding cracks is based on a trick used by antique dealers to find out if their collectible figurines or precious porcelain vases have unseen cracks. Knock on the pot and listen for a ring or a thud. If the tone doesn't carry or ring slightly, then there is a crack in it somewhere. If the sound rings and there is a slight echo, that means the container is solid and doesn't have any cracks. This technique works on all pottery, china, or ceramic pieces and can help you find hidden cracks.

Planting a Broken-Pot Garden

Once you have your broken pot assembled, you can determine what plants will fit into the pockets that you created. Anchor the top bed with a larger tree at the back of the top level. The smaller pockets will need drought-tolerant plants, or at least plants that are horticulturally matched. In this example, a miniature sweet flag paired well with golden baby tears and bits of moss to make a moisture-loving garden. The plants in the top bed of the pot will need regular watering.

Size Matters

If you are planting a large broken pot, plant it in place. Once the pot is filled with soil it will be heavy, and the distribution of the pot's weight will be unequal, with the back side being the heaviest, making it tricky to move. This may seem trivial, but if you are not prepared for the unbalanced weight when you pick up the pot for the first time it might slip out of your hands.

So much can
happen in such
a tiny space.

PROJECT
BREAK YOUR OWN BROKEN POT

In this project you will learn how to break apart a pot almost exactly where you want it broken. By using a hammer and tapping on the pottery in a deliberate way, you put stress on that spot, causing the pottery to weaken and eventually crack. This is similar to taking the hammer and whacking the pottery to break it, but here you do it more intentionally and in small increments so that instead of smashing it, you crack it. Tap up and down the line where you want the pottery to break and you will spread the stress, weaken a bigger area, and cause the whole piece to eventually break off.

Once the pot is reassembled, plant the crevices with small plants to match the scale.

TOOLS AND MATERIALS

Ceramic or earthenware pot

Large towel

Marker

Hammer

Two or three 4-inch nursery pots

Scissors

Silicone glue

INSTRUCTIONS

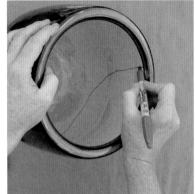

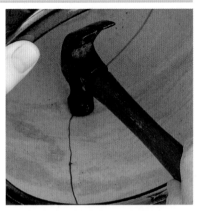

1 Use the marker to draw a line inside the pot where you want to break off a piece. You may not get a break exactly on the line, so leave some margin for error. Lay the pot down on the large towel to keep the pot from getting scratched and to muffle the sound of your taps because they may sound loud.

2 Using a light tap with the hammer, tapping 1 to 2 inches apart, begin to hammer along the line, going back and forth a few times to try to direct the crack as best as you can.

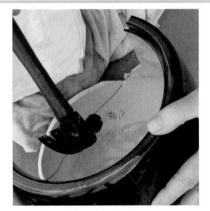

3 Tap along the first 6 to 8 inches of the line, paying more attention to the lip of the pot where you want the crack to start. As you grow more confident with your taps, you can slowly and gradually tap the hammer against the pot a bit harder. Once you hear the ring of your tapping change to a dull thud, you will know the pot is cracked. Move on to the next section of the line and start tapping.

4 Eventually the piece will fall off. Repeat the process for smaller areas if you want to take more off, but be gentler with your taps to get more control.

5 Now play around with the nursery pot and the largest piece of broken pottery. Hold up the broken pieces inside the pot to figure out how they can be glued together. The nursery pot should support the broken piece as much as it can. Rearrange the nursery pot and the largest shard until you are satisfied with how they fit together.

6 Use the marker to mark the spots where the broken piece and the walls of the pot meet. This is where you will glue them together.

7 Using scissors, cut the nursery pot on an angle to fit snugly with the pottery pieces if needed. Keep fitting the pieces together to see how they will be mounted before you start to glue them.

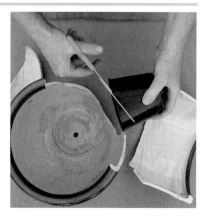

8 Start gluing from the bottom and work toward the top. Glue the nursery pot to the bottom, inside the ceramic container. Glue the pottery shards to the sides of the container. Lay the pot on its side so the pieces stay in place while the glue dries. Let dry completely in stages if the pot and parts will not stay in place while the glue is setting.

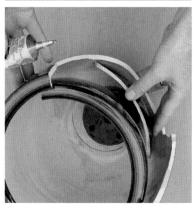

9 Glue the small piece in the front gap in the same way. Now you have a container to start planting.

GET A GRIP

When you move the planted broken-pot garden, do not pick it up by the glued front sides. Move it by the back side of the container only. Make sure you have a good grip on it before you pick it up because the weight will be significantly changed, as the back side will be much heavier than the front side.

CACHEPOTS AND VASES

Fast and Fun Miniature Gardening

Plants add life to any home. You can hire a top interior design professional to create a perfect scheme for your personality and lifestyle. You can live in an award-winning interior, designed and color-coordinated with top-quality drapes, rugs, and upholstery. You can spend thousands of dollars on furniture and fixtures. But if you don't have a plant in the room, it simply lacks life. Plants help brighten your space, improve air quality, reduce stress, remind you of your connection with Mother Nature, and create a more relaxing environment for you.

Despite all the advantages that indoor plants bring to a home, many people are intimidated by them because of the maintenance they require and the occasional mess they make. The idea of lugging a pot and soil indoors, planting on a kitchen floor, finding a place to recycle the plastic pots, and store the soil and tools can foil anyone's desire to nurture plants indoors. Many condominiums and apartments don't have a sunny spot for a container, much less a place to make the mess. Here are some easy solutions for making a simple miniature garden.

Simplified miniature gardening expands on cachepot gardening. Cachepots are decorative containers that are large enough to hold a plant in its original

A maidenhair fern adds a soft and delicate touch.

nursery pot. You drop the whole plant, pot and all, into a cachepot for an instant dose of garden loveliness. Cachepots often don't have drainage holes, but that's okay because to water the plant you simply lift it out, still in its nursery pot, then water it in your sink and let it stand and drain. Once the water has drained you return the plant to the cachepot. If the plant expires, simply plop in a new plant. It's easy-peasy with no muss or fuss! A miniature garden made with a cachepot is an easy way to introduce the joy of a miniature garden into any home anywhere, especially a place where a regular miniature garden might not be allowed.

Another approach to simplified miniature gardening is planting a vase with a cutting in a container. Vases can give you a much deeper vessel to house plant cuttings while they root or to simply enjoy them as water plants. The size and shape of the vase you use will depend upon the size and shape of the container, so choose them both at the same time, holding them up at eye level to get an idea of how they will look together. A vase in a pretty color can be sunk into pebbles in the container and made to look like a big urn in a miniature scene. Plant cuttings placed in water in a plain glass vase, or a clean bottle, and buried all the way down to the collar or lip will make cuttings look like they are planted. A miniature chair, small rock, or piece of driftwood can hide the lip of the bottle. Thrift shops and secondhand stores often have a wide selection of vases in all shapes, colors, and sizes.

To begin, as with any type of indoor gardening, consider the space your container will inhabit. The size of the space will determine what size and shape of cachepot or container you can use. A small windowsill in the bathroom or a bedside table can house only a container, so the vase-and-plant-cutting version of this idea is better suited for those spots. The cachepot version needs a larger, brightly lit spot and is perfect for a coffee table, kitchen counter, or plant stand in front of a living-room window.

If your home receives little or no natural light, think about placing a small table lamp with a plant-friendly bulb next to the little scene. Grow bulbs that can fit into any kind of light fixture are available at indoor-plant shops, hardware stores, or online.

Plants and Cuttings

Small indoor plants can be found at garden centers, florist shops, big-box stores, and sometimes even at grocery stores that have a floral department. Look for leafy plants that have a bit of flair, or with foliage that spreads beyond the pot's edge or drapes down. Rigid upright plants, like tropical succulents, tend to look too static for this idea.

If you like to dote on your plants, choose a moisture-loving plant like a maidenhair fern, a light and airy plant that can lend a tropical look to your scene. Next to a miniature accessory, the leaves of a maidenhair fern seem big and lush. Other water-loving suggestions include pileas, colorful polka dot plants, African violets, button ferns, or any kind of tropical fern for that matter.

If you have a busy lifestyle and need a plant that is a little forgiving of a missed day or two of watering, try pothos, ponytail palms, spider plants, dracenas, or a wandering Jew. Air plants are also low-maintenance and can add an intriguing element to a scene. Using different plants can change a scene dramatically.

A tiny sedum cutting left to root next to a retro porch chair and birdbath.

A cachepot garden three ways.

Kalanchoe.

Dracena.

Maidenhair fern.

For vases, use plants that can be left to root to make more plants, like a pothos vine, spider plants, begonias, or coleus. Evergreen conifer or broadleaf branches can sometimes last several weeks in a vase. Colorful willow branches will liven up seasonal greens in the winter, and your favorite herbs, like mint, basil, and rosemary, can be cut and kept in a vase within reach on the kitchen counter for a few days at a time. For a tiny vase, one small succulent tip or a tiny conifer cutting is perfect next to a wee chair and little rock.

As with bouquets of flowers, the more complicated an arrangement, the shorter its lifespan. Make sure the stems that are below the waterline are stripped clean of leaves. A simple branch or three from the same plant can be just as charming as a composition of flowers.

Easy-Peasy Maintenance

Simplified miniature gardens need very little maintenance: just water the plants regularly and top off the vases with water from time to time. The pebbles will get dusty after a while; you can blow the dust off every now and then. The vases will need cleaning too; how often will depend upon what plants you are using. If the water in the vase gets really murky, corral the pebbles by pouring them onto a sheet of newspaper, a baking sheet, or into a box and remove the vase to clean it. If there's a stubborn algae rim or sediment stuck inside the vase, soak it in warm water and dish soap for a couple of hours. Then, using a knife tip wrapped in a dishrag, scrub the scum off the sides gently.

A pothos cutting in a vase stands in for a miniature tropical palm.

MAKE A SCENE

The materials for a miniature vase or cachepot garden consist of a container, a plant or cutting, pebbles, and a miniature accessory or two. It's a simple concept, but the right combinations can deliver endless charm.

In general, cachepots are large enough to fit the 4-inch or 1-quart black nursery pots that plants come in at nurseries and garden centers. When you're shopping for a cachepot, take your potted plant with you, or a pot that's the same size as the one your potted plant comes in, to be sure that it will fit inside the cachepot. Some cachepots appear to be the right size but may be shaped in a way that will not allow the nursery pot to sink down below the rim and out of view. Your favorite independent garden center should have a selection of plants, containers, and cachepots; florist shops usually have a small selection of cachepots to choose from, too.

Before you go shopping for cachepots or vases, look in your own cupboards; more than likely you already have a nice bowl that suits your decor and will make a great starting point. The bottom container can be a big serving dish, a plant container, a water bowl, or an antique basin. This container does not need a hole in the bottom; if it has one, put a piece of tape over it to contain the pebbles.

↑ Choose a vase, container, and accessories in complementary colors to make a pretty scene.

A bench, a birdcage, and air plants come together nicely in this inviting scene.

Styling the Scene

The scale of the accessories you use in your composition will depend on the size of the bowl or container. Follow the same general guidelines that you would for gardening in miniature: in a container that's more than 10 inches in diameter, use large-size accessories, and in a container that's 10 inches or smaller, use medium-size accessories

With the right combinations, a simplified miniature garden can evoke a range of atmospheres. Here are three gardens that consist of the same components, but evoke entirely different personalities.

TROPICAL ISLAND DREAM A colorful, Malaysian papier-mâché bowl found at a local thrift store inspired this tropical island scene. The wonderful pattern and texture of the dish, combined with the golden-colored vase, conjures warm tropical breezes and deep blue skies. The simple shapes contrast nicely with each other: the wide, shallow bowl is accentuated by the tall calming, gentle shape of the vase. The glowing yellow glass and the solid pattern swirling around the bowl play off each other and increase the exotic-ness of the scene. The pothos vine cuttings are a perfect way to soften the silhouette of the vase and bring the eye down to the real focal point in front. The olive green garden chair instantly delivers the miniature scale and the peaceful atmosphere. The air plants in the pots, the driftwood, and the other, single air plant that looks like an agave shrub finish off the scene

GOTHIC GARDEN You can have a lot of fun developing different themes to make this idea more challenging for yourself, or to customize it for a gift. In this simplified

Transport yourself to the tropics.

A soft color-palette lightens the heavy stone planter.

miniature garden, the rigid stone bowl conjures cement walls around the garden. The faux-aged glass cachepot mimics stained-glass windows and looks gothic or medieval in style. Because parts of the glass cachepot are painted metallic, the other accessories (the bench, birdcage, and hook) are painted metallic to match. The airy maidenhair fern looks like a big patio tree and the branches hanging down on either side softens the hard texture of the glass and stone.

A TWEE GARDEN Now here is a good reason to get those cute little antique candy dishes out of the closet and onto the mantel! The vase used here is a glass ginseng bottle sunk into micro pebbles. The tip of a sedum plant is a perfect cutting for the vase. The small rocks and driftwood give the arrangement a beachy atmosphere; all that's missing are waves lapping on the beach.

A twee garden.

A garden in a candy dish.

GUERRILLA GARDENING

"Quick! Here comes a car! Hide!" Okay, when was the last time you felt like an eleven-year-old allowed to stay out past dark with the other kids? The exhilaration of getting away with something that isn't completely permissible was just thrilling and empowering. Guerrilla gardening can bring back memories of the harmless, fun times of your childhood and make you feel like a kid again. Just ignore the stares if you get caught doing it.

Guerrilla gardening is a bit rebellious because it involves planting on abandoned land that is not being cared for, or on private property. Around the country, guerrilla gardens have shown up on parking strips and roundabouts, around poles, and just about anywhere you can scratch a piece of earth, add some soil, and plant. It's a great way to beautify a neighborhood that needs a little love and elbow grease.

And then there is pothole gardening, which is just what it sounds like. People plant a small plant in a pothole and put a miniature accessory next to it to make an impromptu miniature garden scene. Gardening in potholes sounds like working in the middle of a street, but ideally the pothole would be out of harm's way of cars; for example, perhaps it's next to a sewer grate, just inside an alley, or in between some broken concrete on the sidewalk.

A fun surprise for passersby.

This project is a blend of these two public-gardening options. It's s an idea whose components can fit in a bag and be taken anywhere and, with a little practice, can be executed in minutes. Be warned that you may get a daring James Bond–like feeling as you work, but it will add to the fun of creating a surprise spot of sunshine to brighten someone's day.

This Is Your Mission, If You Choose to Accept It

If you are curious about mini guerrilla gardening, remember that the garden will need maintenance. There isn't much sense in going to all this trouble if you are not going to help the garden survive. By carefully adhering to the "right plant for the right place" maxim you can make your guerrilla garden easier to maintain. And by keeping it small and nearby, you will find it easier to water more often. If you have a dog, you'll have the perfect excuse to take a walk and visit your little creation.

Start with a reconnaissance mission. Scout locations beforehand to find the right spot to plant. Use common sense: do not even *think* about planting up the parking strip in front of the home of that really cranky neighbor down the street. Instead, look for a place you know has been abandoned for a while, one that won't get in anybody's way or bother anybody. It must be a place where no one will mind if there is a little improvement going

233

on. Look for gaps in the asphalt, missing pieces in the sidewalk, or bare spots alongside a building for places to plant and run.

For legitimate guerrilla gardening in public places, ask permission at a school, library, community center, or church in your area. There is a good chance they will smile and say, "Yes, please!" Then look for unused or under-used planters that you can easily take advantage of. Look for unused corners in a garden bed and underneath trees, or perhaps there is an empty place in the middle of a garden bed just beckoning for a little bit of miniature magic.

Assess the Location

Once you find the right spot, assess what you need to bring to the site to make the garden. Is there some soil already there to plant? What condition is the soil in? Is it compacted dirt? Is there barely any dirt there? Remember that soil is dark brown, full of little bark pieces and small chunks of compost, and has a wonderful earthy smell. Dirt is gray, lifeless, and dead looking with no smell. If the soil is impenetrable, see if there is room for you to mound up new soil to plant on top of it. If there is, you will have to estimate how much soil to bring to the site. If there are weeds, pulling them first will help to churn up the soil before you plant.

Does the spot get rain? This would mean a lot less maintenance in the rainy months; you would only have to remember to water in the dry months. Watering, however, is an opportunity to practice your covert gardening skills. For example, bend down and pretend to tie your shoe and give the garden some water from your water bottle. Or sit down next to your tiny plot to take a fake phone call and to pull a weed or two and rehydrate the soil. Wear sunglasses, stay calm, and remember your prime directive: the mission to spread garden goodness throughout the land.

A little public park.

Keep in mind that you can build a guerrilla garden gradually; it doesn't have to be done all at once. You may want to start small right now, with possibly a ground-cover, some soil, and a miniature bench. If that works and you are enjoying the routine, you can think about adding trees, shrubs, and a pathway. Start simple at first: a basic garden design is easier to maintain. Then retreat, slowly, without any sudden moves. This is guerrilla gardening, remember?

Just the Plants, Ma'am, Just the Plants

Now that you know where you are going to plant your guerrilla garden, think about what plants will work in that spot. Figure out how much sun the spot gets and narrow the list accordingly. Then consider the shorter plants first because tall ones may stick out too much or grow over a sidewalk and trip people. You're growing a garden, not a lawsuit. Consider rugged plants with bendable branches that won't break. Structured but delicate plants like sedums or hens and chicks can be damaged in one step, anything thorny wouldn't be very kind, and stiff branches may accidentally scratch an ankle and cause someone harm.

Choose drought-tolerant plants for your guerrilla garden because the plants will still need a full year of care before you leave it to fend for itself. Start with a good-size planting hole and use organic compost to plant it. Water it deeply and infrequently throughout the first year to teach the garden to find water on its own. But, like all drought-tolerant plants in any full-size garden, these will need your help and your water to survive if the area experiences any excessive heat waves or drought.

Taller drought-tolerant plants with bendable branches that make great miniature garden plants may sound like a hurdle, but when you start to think about it, more options will emerge. Some examples are dwarf heather, 'Abbott's Pygmy' dwarf hemlock, ground-cover junipers, dwarf woolly yarrow, sea thrift, dianthus, and dwarf mondo grass. Miniature garden bedding plants that can withstand some traffic and drought conditions include thymes, bugleweed, miniature daisies, Kenilworth ivy, and brass buttons.

Accessorizing the Guerrilla Garden

The ideal accessory size for this guerrilla garden is in the large-size scale because this size allows the accessory to be seen from a distance. Smaller scale accessories tend to get lost in full-size gardens, visually and physically. Most people will look at your guerrilla garden from a standing position of five to six feet away, so the large-size accessories will be noticeable. Other people will get down for a closer look; reward them with smaller details, or something that is hidden from the higher-up view, like a squirrel or tiny fairy house. A premade patio is optional and can be quickly installed. If you have time, create a quick pebble patio, or build a custom permanent patio if time allows.

Tucking a charming miniature garden in a public place is an act of faith, but don't get frustrated if it walks away. Start with one or two accessories that you can afford to lose. The main culprits are usually children playing near the garden with parents who don't notice that the child has taken an accessory. If there are a lot of kids in the area you are going to plant, think about an unstaked accessory that's not sharp or pointy, for safety's sake.

When to Execute the Guerrilla Garden

The best time to plant aligns with the best time to plant a full-size garden: in the fall before temperatures dip to freezing. The cool temperatures and rains in autumn will help you maintain the garden, and the plants will have several months to adjust to their new home before the springtime growing period. You can plant at another time, but you'll need to give the guerrilla garden a little more attention to help it get growing.

If you have no choice but to plant in hot weather, watering-in the plants helps them get situated. This means digging the planting hole, filling it up with water, letting it drain, filling it with water again, waiting for most of the water to be absorbed into the hole, and then planting. Make sure you put fresh compost around the root ball, eliminate any air pockets by gently working the soil around the plant's roots, and water it again. Water the surrounding soil as well. Applying any kind of mulch afterward will help to slow down the water evaporation.

PROJECT
SHARING MINIATURE GARDEN FUN

For this guerrilla-gardening mission, there was room in this school's front garden bed for a few trees and several groundcovers. The soil in the garden bed was a good mix of compost and bark mulch, so no extra soil was needed, leaving room in the carry bag for more plants. The number of plants used in this example will need to be adjusted for your mission. Bring along a copy of *Gardening in Miniature*; it provides you with a pretext if anyone asks what you're doing.

TOOLS AND MATERIALS

Four different trees and shrubs in 4-inch pots, different textures and growth shapes

Four groundcover plants

Two garden benches

Premade miniature patio

Mini pavers

Small shovel

Gloves

Kneeling pad

INSTRUCTIONS

1 To make sure the plants do not get squashed in the bag, put them in a cardboard box, then put the box in a bag so everything will stay in place when you are carrying it to the location.

2 First, pull any weeds and remove any debris from the soil, and make any necessary soil amendments.

3 Plant the guerrilla garden like any other miniature garden: plant the larger trees at the back of the space first. Layer down from there with shrubs and bedding plants.

4 Lay the patio, path, and accent pieces such as boulders and furniture.

5 It will be a few years until the plants start to hide the sign's message.

MINIATURE SCALES

Large size or 1-inch scale
1 inch = 1 foot
A 6-foot person is 6 inches tall.

Medium size or ½-inch scale
½ inch = 1 foot
A 6-foot person is 3 inches tall.

Small size or ¼-inch scale
¼ inch = 1 foot
A 6-foot person is 1½ inches tall.

METRIC CONVERSIONS

INCHES	CENTIMETERS
¼	0.6
½	1.3
¾	1.9
1	2.5
2	5.1
3	7.6
4	10
5	13
6	15
7	18
8	20
9	23
10	25

FEET	METERS
1	0.3
2	0.6
3	0.9
4	1.2
5	1.5
6	1.8
7	2.1
8	2.4
9	2.7
10	3
20	6
30	9
40	12

TEMPERATURES

$$°C = 5/9 \times (°F-32)$$

$$°F = (9/5 \times °C) + 32$$

RECOMMENDED READING

Miniature Making

Dodge, Martin, and Venus Martin. 1989. *Making Miniatures in 1/12 Scale*. England: David & Charles Craft Book. An inspirational book filled with instructional how-tos and detailed diagrams. The book explains how to make room boxes, furniture, houses and more, and includes a chapter on how to create a secret dollhouse garden.

Freeman, Jane. 2002. *The Art of the Miniature: Small Worlds and How to Make Them*. New York: Potter Craft. Packed with information about making artistic miniatures and unique shadowboxes, this book will spark your imagination. You will never look at a tiny object the same way again. The author uses Bic lighters for turnstiles, postage stamps as paintings, and pencil tops for cups. Other artists are highlighted throughout the book.

Gray, Freida. 2005. *Making Miniature Gardens*. 4th edition. East Sussex: Guild of Master Craftsman Publications Ltd. Features dollhouse miniature gardens (artificial) only. The book is filled with projects for crafting almost every aspect of the garden, including soil, furniture, walls, and flowers, and a potting bench and more.

Mulvany, Kevin, and Susie Rogers. 2008. *Magnificent Miniatures: Inspiration and Technique for Grand Houses on a Small Scale*. London: Batsford. An excellent book on dollhouse miniatures that takes you on the authors' journey through making their incredible and historically accurate palaces, room boxes, and houses. This book is a treat for the serious or armchair miniaturist.

Nisbett, Jean. 2005. *A Beginners' Guide to the Dolls' House Hobby, Revised and Expanded Edition*. East Essex: Guild of Master Craftsman Publications. Dive into dollhouse detailing with Jean Nisbett as she demonstrates a wide variety of techniques for working in miniature. There is a handy chapter on period styles that lists architectural styles and color palettes. Jean steps through each room in the dollhouse, teaching historical accuracy from each era.

Schramer, Mike, and Debbie Schramer. 2015. *Fairy House: How to Make Amazing Fairy Furniture, Miniatures, and More from Natural Materials*. Sanger, CA: Familius LLC. If you love everything fairy, enjoy crafting with natural materials, and need ideas and inspiration, then this book is for you. Many of the projects are repetitive but are perfect for kids, beginner artists, or for armchair fairy crafting.

Working with Polymer Clay

Carlson, Maureen. 2006. *Fairies, Gnomes & Trolls: Create a Fantasy World in Polymer Clay*. Cincinnati, OH: North Light Books. A quirky but fun book about creating a wide variety of fantasy creatures out of polymer clay, this book covers the use of armatures, building techniques, and it includes permission to sculpt from your imagination.

Dewey, Katherine. 2008. *Creating Lifelike Figures in Polymer Clay: Tools and Techniques for Sculpting Realistic Figures*. New York: Potter Craft. A wonderful book that focuses on sculpting the human body out of polymer clay. This is a great reference to have on hand if you want to sculpt a face or a hand. The techniques can be extended to any kind of clay work. A section on making your own tools for sculpting is especially informative.

More on Gardening Small

Aiello, Amy, and Kate Bryant. 2011. *Terrarium Craft: Create 50 Magical, Miniature Worlds*. Portland, OR: Timber Press. This is a beautiful book that teaches the basics of growing plants under glass. The projects are varied and simple yet inspiring. You will be looking around your house for terrarium ideas after reading it.

Calvo, Janit. 2013. *Gardening in Miniature: Create Your Own Tiny Living World*. Portland, OR: Timber Press. This is the best-selling and most comprehensive book on the hobby. Practical advice on scale, plant selection, containers, and growing information is included accompanied by wonderful photographs that will delight and inspire you. Eight projects are included to get you started growing in miniature.

Ee, Su Chin. 2003. *Creating Bonsai Landscapes: 18 Miniature Garden Projects*. North Adams, MA: Storey Publishing. If the art of bonsai intrigues you, you will love this beautiful book based in the art of penjing. The projects are very inspiring for the miniature gardener. Construct landscapes complete with waterfalls, ponds, and mountains, or grow and shape trees for your wee landscape. You'll find the techniques fascinating and the growing methods very doable. Ideal plants for each project are listed throughout the book.

Martin, Annie. 2015. *The Magical World of Moss Gardening*. Portland, OR: Timber Press. You won't need another book on moss because this one has everything you need to get you growing moss in your area. Chapters include a tour of moss gardens, the botany and history of moss, a list of mosses to know and grow, and planting and designing with moss. A chapter on maintenance and troubleshooting is included.

Sengo, Zenaida. 2014. *Air Plants: The Curious World of Tillandsias*. Portland, OR: Timber Press. Beautifully photographed and complete with all the information you need to grow, craft with, decorate with, or wear air plants.

For More Crafty Fun in the Garden

Rose, Stephanie. 2015. *Garden Made: A Year of Seasonal Projects to Beautify Your Garden & Your Life*. Boston, MA: Roost Books. A fun book full of different and doable garden projects that are sorted by the seasons so you can find a project to suit your crafty urges quickly and easily. Great photos in each project demonstrate how to make an easy garden chandelier and quick garden gifts; ways to grow plants in unusual places; these are just a few of the many projects included in this book.

SHOPPING RESOURCES

BLICK'S ART SUPPLY
dickblick.com
Carries Utrecht acrylic paints, which are inexpensive and high-quality acrylic paints. Blick's also carries paintbrushes and Paverpol, the textile hardener used in a few of the projects in this book.

MICHAELS CRAFTS
michaels.com
Michaels is a national chain store that carries a comprehensive selection of craft supplies, including glues, brushes, dowels, floral wire, and paintbrushes as well as wooden miniatures that you can customize.

PAVERPOL
paverpolusa.com
Paverpol manufactures the textile hardener used in a few of the projects. Visit the website for more information about the product.

TWO GREEN THUMBS MINIATURE GARDEN CENTER
twogreenthumbs.com
Find a wide variety of trees, plants, and bedding plants for gardening in miniature here, as well as unusual miniatures, kits, and inspiration.

YOUR LOCAL HARDWARE STORE
Stop at your local hardware store for wood hardener, exterior wood glues, dowels, sandpaper, and disposable paintbrushes.

YOUR LOCAL INDEPENDENT GARDEN CENTER
Visit your local independent garden center to see what plants are best for your area. They may also have fairy-garden miniatures for customizing.

ACKNOWLEDGMENTS

A huge thank you to Juree Sondker, Eve Goodman, Sarah Milhollin, and everyone at Team Timber, for their hard work in assembling all the parts and pieces from my head into one book. Thank you to photographer Kate Baldwin, for your patience in working in miniature and in my full-size garden. Also my appreciation to Lesley Bruynesteyn, who made sure that all the details work.

A loving thank you to my husband, maid, cook, gopher, therapist, mechanic, laborer, assistant, partner, shoulder, and best friend, Steve, who held down the fort during this process. It couldn't have been done without you.

And a warm thank you to my agent, Rita Rosenkranz, for believing in me from the beginning, and planting me in garden history.

PHOTOGRAPHY CREDITS

Photos by Kate Baldwin appear on pages 2, 3, 5, 10–11, 28–29, 30, 32, 33, 34, 38, 42–43, 44, 46, 47 top, 50 top, 53, 54, 56, 57, 58, 59, 62, 66, 67–68, 70 top, 72 right, 74, 76 left, 80–81, 82, 84, 86 top, 87 bottom right, 88, 90, 91, 92–93, 95 left, 97 right, 98, 101 right, 102, 106, 111, 116, 118, 121 left, 124, 126, 127, 128, 129 left, 131 top, 134, 135, 136, 137, 138 right, 141 left, 148 bottom, 149, 160, 162, 163, 164, 168 top, 171, 180, 181, 182, 184–185, 186, 189, 194–195, 196 right, 202–203, 204, 210, 211, 212, 214, 217, 218, 219, 222, 224–225, 226, 227, 228, 229, 230, 231, 232, 234–235.

All other photographs are by Janit Calvo.

INDEX

kalanchoe, 225
Kenilworth ivy, 236
knives, 25, 26
knots, 197

lady fern, 104
lawns in scenes, 117, 127, 128
Lawson's cypress, 217
leaves, 161, 164, 184, 193
light
    grow bulbs, 225
    indoor, 184, 225
    in a work space, 15
lighted archway, step-by-step, 95–97
light strings, step-by-step, 121–123
linesman's pliers, 18
'Little Heath' Japanese andromeda, 104
log border, step-by-step, 168–170
London pride, 104

maidenhair fern, 225, 226, 230
maidenhair vine, 89
maintenance
    accessibility, 151
    guerrilla gardens, 233, 235
    outdoor vs. indoor miniature gardens, 89
    for simplified gardens, 227
materials. *See individual project lists*
meditation altar, step-by-step, 70–71
miniature begonias, 205
miniature daisies, 236
miniature hebe, 193
miniature London pride 'Primuloides', 104
miniature rose 'Charlie Brown', 104
miniature sweet flag, 217
mini miter saw, 25–26
mint, 227
Mod-Podge, 25, 86, 87
mosaic patio, step-by-step, 62–64
moss, 127, 128, 161, 217
Mother's Day theme, 103–114
moving gardens, 136, 217, 221
Muehlenbeckia complexa, 89
mugo pines, 31
    'Slowmound', 193

national themes, 31–79
ninebark, 161
Norfolk pines, 67

ornamental grass, 104, 106
ornament strings, 139
outdoor silicone glue, 20
outer space theme, 181–191

paint
    acrylic artist paint, 22
    color names, listed, 23
    enamel, 22
    latex house paint, 23
    nail polish, 22–23, 39
    spray, 24
    useful types, 22–24
    washes, 22, 33, 47, 59–61
paintbrushes, 24
parahebe 'Delight', 104
parasols, 72–73
park scene, 45–52
parsley, 106
passionflower, 94
pathways, 20, 21, 151, 237
patio mix, 21
patios
    ancient brick, step-by-step, 47–49
    design ideas, 117
    mosaic, step-by-step, 62–64
    setting, 21
    trees for, 55, 230
penjing, 79
peperomias, 205
pileas, 205, 225
pine cones, 147, 161, 181. *See also* cones
pitcher plants, 128
plants
    able to withstand traffic, 236
    for adding age to the garden, 152
    allowing time to grow, 89
    in broken-pot gardens, 215, 217
    for enclosed environments, 205
    frightening, 128
    for guerrilla gardens, 236
    indoor, 184, 223, 225–226
    layering, 152
    leggy, 55, 57, 181, 193
    for miniature gardening, 181
    moisture-loving, 225
    with similar needs, 193, 205, 217
    with small flowers, 103, 104
    strange or alien-looking, 181, 183–184, 193

KATE BALDWIN

JANIT CALVO is an author, artist, miniaturist, blogger, gardener, photographer, and entrepreneur. She gardens with her husband, Steve, in Seattle, Washington, surrounded by her award-winning miniature worlds of all shapes and sizes.

A pioneer of miniature gardening, in 2001 Janit founded Two Green Thumbs Miniature Garden Center, America's first miniature garden store. She is president of the Miniature Garden Society, a place where like-minded miniature gardeners from all over the world can create and connect. Her first book, *Gardening in Miniature: Create Your Own Tiny Living World* (2013), was an instant bestseller.

Find more information and links to her websites, online stores, the Miniature Garden Society, and her popular *Mini Garden Guru* blog at MiniatureGarden.com.